IN SEARCH OF AMERICA

Rvhi Wnf
10 / 6. 2015

WORKS BY ROBERT WOLF

Fiction
Grand Tally

Non-Fiction
The Triumph f Technique:
Jump Start: How to Write from Everyday Life
Story Jazz: A History of Chicago Jazz Styles
Crazeology

Plays
Drfitless Dreams
Heartland Portrait
The Strike at Pullman
Ragnorak

Edited
An American Mosaic
Violence in the Holy Land
Heartland Portrait
River Days
Eating in Place
Ayer y Ahora
Mixed Beans

IN SEARCH OF AMERICA

A Young Man's Quest for Meaning

By
Robert Wolf

RUSKIN PRESS
P.O. Box 10
Decorah, Iowa 52101

1. Memoir 2. American studies. 3. American history
4. America in the 1960s

Ruskin Press
P.O. Box 10
Decorah, IA 52101

This is a work of nonfiction, but some names have been changed.

For Manuel, Hal, Gene, Genie and others
who helped me slong the road.

PART ONE

PROLOGUE

I'm standing in the post office in Nara Visa, New Mexico, the last business in town. Nara Visa's wreckage is apparent from the highway that cuts through this collection of crumbling adobe houses, dilapidated stores, and abandoned café and truck stop.

Eighty years ago Nara Visa was a regional center for cattle shipping. Ranchers within a fifty-mile radius drove their herds to the rail yard where they were loaded on cattle cars and shipped to slaughterhouses. Now the days of the cowboy who lived on a ranch and worked full time are over. Today most cowboys do day work—a day here and a day there.

Standing nearby me at the postal counter is a young man in a Texas style hat (the sides of the brim are molded to curve up), clean jeans and shirt, with a drooping mustache on his upper lip and a wad of snuff beneath his lower lip. The flesh beneath the lower lip protrudes. He is trying to look and act like a cowboy, but his movements and speech are self-conscious.

Without asking his name I know at once who he is: the son of the postal clerk whom I met at the annual Nara Visa Cowboy Gathering about six years ago. I know he is her son because back around five years ago she had told a group of us eating dinner about his ambition. She did not want him to pursue it. Why? I asked. She pointed first to my close friend sitting beside me, Clyde Shepherd, an old-time cowboy and ranch manager, and then pointed to his walker.

Now the clerk's son is living his dream, but the dream of the cowboy is over, as far as steady work goes. Aside from the largest ranches, most cattle operations cannot afford full-time cowboys— or find it more profitable not to hire any.

Like the farmer and the commercial fisherman, the cowboy is a vanishing breed. But it is precisely the vanishing breeds that have held my attention since I first read about them as a kid. I identified these iconic workers as the most representative of Americans. In my young mind, despite their outward differences of speech and other cultural markings, they best expressed what was fundamentally American.

By the time I was sixteen, I was sure there was such a thing as the American soul. My imagination had been fired by American regionalist writings and paintings, and by the hoboing and cross-country treks of people like Carl Sandburg and Jack Kerouac. I determined to go in search of the American soul and look for it, not among businessmen and their wives (I had plenty of exposure to them growing up) but among farmers, ranchers, welders, fishermen, auto mechanics—the working people of America. And not all working people, but those rooted in regional cultures. I suppose I understood intuitively that my search would focus on areas that had been relatively untouched by modernization.

This was a romantic quest, a young person's quest. Not only did I want to travel, I wanted to work every job in the country, live in every town, have conversations with everyone. And so at seventeen, cramped and stifled by my suburban Connecticut community, I ran off and hitchhiked to Ohio to visit my paternal grandparents.

Over the years I continued to travel—driving, hitchhiking, hopping freights, riding buses—back and forth across country. At age 69 I have lived in ten states and had lengthy sojourns in others. I have had more jobs than most people.

Since the summer I hitchhiked to Ohio, I have kept my antennae tuned to the country's cultural backwaters, to cultural survivals from the past. In these backwaters—Hispanic villages, Iowa farms, Texas Panhandle and Tennessee Delta towns—I have found most of my close friends, the people with whom I am most simpatico. To the striving urbanite, I imagine, my friends are merely irrelevancies in the hustling world. Even most of my friend's children do not want to live as their parents did: they want high-paying jobs in tumultuous American cities: they want what everyone else seems to want—the latest technological gadgets, status cars, big houses, a stunning stock portfolio. The list goes on.

This would-be cowboy in Nara Visa is an exception among the children of my friends who grew up in vanishing regional cultures, primarily because the young man's culture fostered his dream, and also because his isolation offered him few opportunities. If his parents had left Nara Visa and moved to Amarillo, he might have become a car mechanic or welder.

My search for distinctly American meanings took me to people and experiences that as a youth I had only read about or seen in the cinema. Over the years I lived and worked on a ranch off and on for four years, taught college composition, wrote features for a big city daily, did office temp work, taught biology in a Brooklyn inner-city school, clerked in a big box store, and more. Each job brought me into contact with very different kinds of people, not just different races and ethnic groups. In the days when I wanted to be a writer but failed to work at the art, a famous writer who knew my ambition told me that someday my experiences would pay off.

Even now, over thirty years since my conversations with the writer, I continue traveling the country, stopping for a week or a month in a city or isolated village. I feel most alive when I am on the move, meeting new folk. I have a need to share these experiences, and as a fractured nation we need to hear one another's voices. Now that fragmentation is the force driving our society, we need more than ever to grasp the common humanity that lies beneath the preconceptions and ignorance that divide us.

I cannot explain my passion for experience and knowledge through nurture or environment, for my parents had little thirst for either. Neither did New Canaan, Connecticut, the town of my adolescence. On the contrary, by their very natures, home and New Canaan were places from which to escape.

Home was a family that threatened and yelled, or simmered with tension. New Canaan was and is a commuter town for New York executives and their families. If it had not been for the stultifying influence of New Canaan, where I lived from age 12 to 17, I doubt that I would have become so passionately independent. A less restrictive culture would not have bred such reaction.

Our family moved to New Canaan in 1957. These were the Eisenhower years. American factories were churning out cars, dishwashers, televisions sets and radios, backyard barbecues, and boxed cereals. The growing white middle-class had wages to spend. Even northern blacks in Detroit and Chicago with unionized factory jobs enjoyed this period of American prosperity. With a prosperous middle class with money to spend, advertising burgeoned. Advertising became a seam in the American fabric, something we took for granted and could even enjoy, especially the radio and television commercials with their perky, upbeat jingles that we could hum or sing to ourselves.

America's consumer culture was burgeoning, but this consumer culture bred conformity, since everyone wanted the same things and some wanted even more. Somehow, we were all supposed to walk lock step. Everyone, including children, was supposed to fit in. The socially adjusted person was likable and therefore liked. He smiled. Ipana toothpaste spread the gospel of happiness through acceptance. The well-adjusted person smiled—the Ipana smile.

New Canaan culture in respect to conformity was especially adamant. But surely New Canaan was no different than other nearby affluent communities like Greenwich, or Darien, or the faraway Shaker Heights or any other town populated with white males who commuted to middle and upper management jobs in American cities.

But New Canaan culture was not only conformist, it was mechanized. New Canaan men lined the station platform, reading the *New York Times* as they waited for their morning trains. In the winter they wore blue, gray or dark brown suits with overcoats and snap-brim hats or homburgs. In warmer weather they wore lighter colored suits. Each weekday morning, as their wives drove them to the station, the station lot filled with slowly moving or stalled cars. The streets outside the station were likewise clogged as train after train arrived. In the evening the process reversed.

Appearances were everything—in dress, speech and choice of friends. Children—excepting those from working class families—were expected to be well groomed and obedient. Housewives had perfectly shellacked hair, and when not shopping or cleaning house, socialized with other housewives while playing golf or bridge. In fact, there were few acceptable ways besides golf and bridge for adults to entertain themselves.

A clean house, a successful husband and bright, obedient children were the New Canaan housewife's pride. A New Canaan housewife could have nothing less than an immaculate home—at all times. My mother even cleaned our home before our maid, Vivian, arrived, lest Vivian tell other women that my mother had less than perfect homemaking skills.

Perfection was the goal in all of life. Life itself was to be lived on a prescribed track. The goal at the end of the track was money, which guaranteed security and respect. After high school came college, then a high paying job. Somewhere along the line one got married and raised a family and the process started over. My father ridiculed our next-door neighbor's son who had gone to India, because it was not only a waste of time but showed an absence of sound values. The boy was lost, confused.

I, too, had fallen off the track. By upper middle-class American standards, by the time I was twenty-one I had thrown away three years of my life, drifting across country. As my father said a few years later, "You've spent enough time with the lower elements of society, now you need to know the upper."

My parents' desire and need for me to conform was an expression of the pressures that had molded them and their generation. Not only was New Canaan's culture highly conformist, it was mechanized, but so was 1960s American culture as a whole. More and more Americans had adapted to the routines that machines and technique were demanding.

The post-war years through the early sixties were a time when technologies were beginning to proliferate in what, forty years later, would become a veritable flood. This mechanized culture, then in its nascent form, grew to encompass all human activity and thereby marginalize all those who clung to old economies and folkways. Technique and the sciences became the handmaidens of business and industry, and those who did not adopt the latest techniques were left behind in the backwaters of American culture. Thus the small farmer was eventually driven to extinction, along with the lumberjack, the cowboy, the commercial fisherman, all occupations demanding relentless physical endurance and risk. By their very nature, these occupations were humanizing, not brutalizing. The men of these occupations took pride in their work and out of each class grew a folk hero: Paul Bunyon among lumberjacks, Pecos Bill among cowboys, Old Stormalong among all times. My mother even cleaned our home before our maid, Vivian, arrived, lest Vivian tell other women that my mother had less than perfect homemaking skills.

Perfection was the goal in all of life. Life itself was to be lived on a prescribed track. The goal at the end of the track was money, which guaranteed security and respect. After high school came college, then a high paying job. Somewhere along the line one got married and raised a family and the process started over. My father ridiculed our next-door neighbor's son who had gone to India, because it was not only a waste of time but showed an absence of sound values. The boy was lost, confused.

I, too, had fallen off the track. By upper middle-class American standards, by the time I was twenty-one I had thrown away three years of my life, drifting across country. As my father said a few years later, "You've spent enough time with the lower elements of society, now you need to know the upper."

My parents' desire and need for me to conform was an expression of the pressures that had molded them and their generation. Not only was New Canaan's culture highly conformist, it was mechanized, but so was 1960s American culture as a whole. More and more Americans had adapted to the routines that machines and technique were demanding.

The post-war years through the early sixties were a time when technologies were beginning to proliferate in what, forty years later, would become a veritable flood. This mechanized culture, then in its nascent form, grew to encompass all human activity and thereby marginalize all those who clung to old economies and folkways. Technique and the sciences became the handmaidens of business and industry, and those who did not adopt the latest techniques were left behind in the backwaters of American culture. Thus the small farmer was eventually driven to extinction, along with the lumberjack, the cowboy, the commercial fisherman, all occupations demanding relentless physical endurance and risk. By their very nature, these occupations were humanizing, not brutalizing. The men of these occupations took pride in their work and out of each class grew a folk hero: Paul Bunyon among lumberjacks, Pecos Bill among cowboys, Old Stormalong among sailors,

John Henry for black workingmen, and Joe Magarac for steel-workers. Each of these folk heroes was supremely competent at his work and capable of superhuman feats. John Henry's battle against the mechanical pile driver, victory and subsequent death, point to what many workingmen must have known would be their eventual fate.

The cowboy in the Nara Visa post office no doubt knows it too, but he is determined to follow his heart. At age seventeen, constricted by parental and societal standards, I packed a suitcase and took a train for New York to follow my own heart and hitch-hike west.

ONE
Santa Fe (Summer 1966)

I was sitting on a wicker rocker on Alan Hay's front porch in Santa Fe. My college buddies, Mac and Alan, were still inside. Mac was asleep and Alan, who stayed under his ratty blankets hours after waking up, was either reading something abstruse in philosophy, or mathematics, or else scheming on a fast fortune. At twenty-one I was the youngest of the three.

Across the road was Hal West's gallery and studio. The three of us had heard of Hal from a western writer we admired and wanted to meet him. I was not thinking of this, though, when Hal's screen door swung open and Hal, a western artist, short and sarto-rial with mustache, dressed in khakis and knit shirt, stepped out-side and looked both ways along the road.

Something flashed, a recognition I have had a few times see-ing certain men, something in their dress, or poise, or speech or all of these tells me these men are complete, that whatever their reality, whatever scope of the world they have set for themselves, they fill it completely, and I knew then that West was such a man. I saw it in his look, his stance, in those few simple movements as he stooped for the newspaper on the narrow dirt sidewalk.

Alan at that moment came out and pitched a "hello" to Har-old and that, as I later thought, was the beginning of my life in

America. Hal said, "Morning, kiddo" and stepped back inside, the screen door thwapping quietly behind him. Alan and I chatted awhile, then he went back inside to his books and I got up and walked across the road to Hal's front door on which a small hand lettered sign said "open." I stepped into a room with a small bed and paintings that covered the walls, one above the other. I peered into the kitchen where Hal sat behind an old, grained wood table. "Come in," he called. I sat down opposite him as naturally as if I had known him from boyhood, sitting around a cast iron stove at a crossroads general store.

Hal handed me a mimeographed paper and asked, "What do you make of this?" The paper claimed to describe certain home-grown communist threats within America. I said, "Might be," but really did not believe the claims. "Makes sense to me," Hal said.

I thought perhaps he was a conspiracy nut, but he was not. That was the one and only time he ever mentioned anything even remotely connected to politics.

Hal asked if I would have breakfast and I said yes. He fried eggs in an old iron skillet and made toast and coffee. His cooking range was an old high-backed wood-burning stove with lids, converted to gas. His coffee pot was huge and blue, speckled with white. The coffee was strong and acidic.

I realized I had entered another world. This was not the world of New Canaan, which was a world of clocks, appointments, deadlines, and responsibilities, a world of serious people. This was something far more real. It was relaxed, but that was because in those days Santa Fe—that portion of it that grew from Hispanic and Indian roots and was nurtured by the early Anglo artists—was not dominated by time. Within a dozen years that would change, but in 1966, at least, I was living outside the strictures of New Canaan.

Mac, Alan, and I had a dinner club at our college, St. John's, to which we invited area artists and writers, one of whom was Jack Schaefer, the author of *Shane*.

While Hal cooked I said, "Jack Schaefer told me and some of my friends about you. And your sons, especially Archie. He spoke very highly of Archie. Said he was one of the last working cowboys in this area."

"Jack Schaefer," Hal mused. "I haven't seen ole Jack in quite a while. So he spoke about Archie."

"Yes."

"Archie's a good boy. He works hard. He runs a little ranch south of here."

Hal told me to get forks, spoons, knives, and plates from the cabinet and drawer in back of me. The plates were old and cracked, no two alike, and the utensils were worn. I laid them out and Hal served the food.

After we ate and were sitting around smoking, the front screen door opened and Alan boomed out, "Is Hal West here?"

"He's in the kitchen," Hal said, and Alan and Mac ambled inside.

"Hello," Mac said.

They stood in the kitchen doorway.

"Come on in. Pull up some chairs, boys, and set down," Hal said.

The two sat and introduced themselves and Hal said, "Nice to know you boys."

"We've heard of you," Alan said.

"Is that so?" Hal said. "Would you like some coffee?"

"Sure."

"Just get yourselves some cups from that cabinet," Hal said, nodding to indicate it.

"Are those your paintings in the front room?" Mac asked.

"They are," Hal said. "Have a look."

We looked around the front room, admiring the paintings, which were mostly of a by-gone era and mostly of Oklahoma and New Mexico—paintings of an abandoned homestead, cotton pickers, farmers plowing behind mules, a hitchhiker sitting on a suitcase alongside an empty highway, country people standing outside a frame house at night with the stars out. The paintings told stories.

When we stepped back inside the kitchen, Hal said, "Do all three of you go to St. John's?"

I had already told Hal that I did.

"Yes."

"Well, that's good. Do you expect you're educated enough to play a game of dominoes?"

"It's a game?" I asked.

"Yes," he said. "Would you like to try it?"

"Sure," we said, and Hal rolled back his chair, opened the table drawer, took out a small cardboard box and dumped the dominoes across the table. "Get 'em all upside down so the dots don't show." We did that. "Now I mix 'em up real good so no one with a sharp eye and a dishonest nature can cheat." Then he told us how to play.

Such an encounter between an elderly adult and three youths, let alone one youth, would not have occurred in New Canaan, or Darien, or Greenwich. Adults in these towns were serious. It would have been beneath the dignity of an ad agency account executive to play dominoes with his son and the sons' friends. Or for a mother to play with her daughter and her friends. Adults lived in a world apart. In fact, my father did most of the time, literally, traveling on business across the states and in Europe.

Life in Santa Fe was fairly spontaneous and somewhat disorderly. People, of course, had jobs but there was a sense of continuous socializing, particularly in bars. If you took a notion to visit someone, you did not call, you just showed up. The formalities of New Canaan and like towns did not exist in Santa Fe. At the time I arrived, in 1965, not a few of the wealthy were a part of the bohemian scene. Santa Fe was not exactly a seamless fabric, but there was still a lot of socializing across ethnic and social lines. At Hal West's home and studio, any number of characters might show up.

From that first meeting I spent every day for the next three months at Hal's, sometimes writing, sometimes painting, sometimes drinking coffee and listening to the people who dropped by. Meeting these people was a big part of my education. None of them would have been at home in New Canaan or any other bourgeois enclave.

***

The summer we met Hal was a summer of discoveries: meeting

artists and visiting their studios; seeing colorful Mexican folk art for the first time; meeting Hispanics and Indians; learning about a city that was so different from any other we had known.

When I was alone that summer I would wonder, "What are Alan and Mac up to?" That summer we all lived with a constant sense of anticipation and excitement. What was next? Who might we meet? What might we see or learn?

We were playing melodramas Friday and Saturday nights at the Tiffany Saloon in Cerrillos. The Tiffany was a survival from this 1880s former mining town, about thirty miles from Santa Fe. A few hundred residents lived among a handful of the remaining old buildings.

I said to Hal, "The three of us are acting in a melodrama in Cerrillos. We have a show tonight. Would you be our guest for dinner and the play?"

"A melodrama?" Hal said excitedly. "Why, hell yes, I will."

We decided we would eat at the saloon. Alan and Mac left, while I stayed with Hal.

"You know, kiddo," Hal said to me as he dressed, "these impromptu parties are some of the jolliest." He put on an English tweed cap, a tweed sports jacket, and a green wool tie. He looked natty. To complete the picture he grabbed a cane.

We crossed the street, got into Alan's car, and roared off for Cerrillos. Hal and I strolled around the dusty streets of this near ghost town as sunset approached, arm in arm. "You don't think it's odd my taking your arm, do you?" Hal asked.

"Not at all," I said.

"I'm not quite as firm or as strong on my legs as I once was. You might have to keep me from falling."

At the time Hal came to the show we were presenting two short plays I had written. My favorite, *The Authentic Life and Death of Wild River Jack Johnson*, features a cowardly bad man and braggart inspired by a St. John's classmate.

After his first visit, Hal came to every performance. He cheered the villains and belittled the heroes.

Primed with drinks they bought before the show, or from waitresses who constantly worked the aisles, the audience yelled advice and warnings to the hero. They threw peanuts at me, the villain in both pieces, and once even threw such a continuous hail of peanuts pin-pricking my face that I walked off stage, afraid for my eyes. (Later that same night one customer even threw a Coke bottle at me.) Mac was upset, wanted to know why I left; I explained but it did not penetrate.

Those were great evenings on stage, roaring lines, losing lines, howling, shouting, hamming for the great crowds that poured in from the restaurant after they had dined. Standing at the crowded bar before the show or between plays or moving through the diners packed at tables, I felt the rooms electric with excitement.

We asked Hal if he would make a poster for us. With brush and ink he drew a pretty little heroine, mouth open, being strangled by a villain who has his big hands around her throat. Standing beside the villain is the citified hero, holding a gun pointed at the villain's head. Mac learned to make silk screen prints and made multiple copies with black ink on brown wrapping paper, which we posted around Santa Fe.

From that day on I began spending most of my mornings in Hal's studio, typing stories and notes in the back room. In the afternoons I would sit with him in his kitchen to meet the visitors who stopped by for a chat or a game of dominoes. A few were artists and writers who had lived in Santa Fe for decades. Some were well-known characters; others were simply tourists. A big part of my Santa Fe education began in Hal's studio.

A bigger part of it came in the evenings when Hal and I would walk downtown for our toddies. Around four-thirty most days he would don a tie and jacket, stick a handkerchief in his jacket pocket, pick up his cane and off we would stroll arm in arm down Canyon Road, headed for La Fonda.

La Fonda is a grand hotel in downtown Santa Fe, on a corner of the Plaza. Inside is a big red-tiled lobby with plastered pillars, large Spanish colonial chairs and sofas spaced in groups around the pillars.

In those days La Fonda had a dark quiet bar where we would sit at a table and watch people. There was always a side table with a big steaming tray of freshly peeled hot green peppers mixed with melted cheese. I would heap two plates with cheese and peppers and another with taco chips. That was our dinner.

Almost always there were people there who knew Hal and would sit and talk with us. If we did not know anyone we would play a game Hal taught me. He would say, "I'll bet you that the next person that walks in here is a single man," or else a woman with a husband, or whatever. And we would throw two nickels on the table and wait. Or else we would pick a table of drinkers and try to guess their occupations. Hal might say, "I'll bet that ole boy with the red tie over there sells insurance." We would drop our nickels on the table and I would walk over and say, "Excuse me, sir. My friend and I just placed a little bet on you. He says you sell insurance and I say you own a pharmacy." Almost always the guy would laugh and say we had both lost. (Occasionally one of us actually did win.) Then he would tell us what he did, and if his table were next to ours it usually started a conversation and Hal would tell them he was an artist and show his portfolio of prints and drawings—if he had brought them.

The prints came from the Cowboy Calendars that Hal had produced years earlier, which featured a woodcut for each month. I have one framed cut that Hal's son, Jerry, gave me after his father died. It depicts a cowboy in the air, legs spraddled wide as he is tossed over the front end of a pitching bronc. The prints were inexpensive and someone at the table usually bought one.

After two drinks we would walk slowly across the Plaza. The Plaza is a block square and in those days was nothing more than packed earth with cement walks running from its four corners to the obelisk at the center, which was surrounded by circular cement seating.

Sometimes we would stop to drink at the Plaza Bar, which was a loud and sometimes raucous meeting place for a cross-section of Santa Fe, from Mexican-Americans and Indians to artists and white-collar workers.

The nearby Palace Restaurant was altogether different—a subdued restaurant and bar which offered steak and lobster. The Palace had an old ornate back bar and was decorated with florid red wallpaper and paintings in flouncy gold-tinted frames. The décor was inspired by a famous bordello that had once occupied the site.

A black-haired, mustached piano player, Jim Dolan, sang and played old-time, often rowdy songs. Whenever we came in Jim would boom, "Hello Hal WEST!" while continuing to play. During breaks, he would come and sit with us.

The last but best bar Hal introduced me to was Claude's, a short walk up Canyon Road from his studio. Claude's was the heartbeat of Santa Fe's bohemian culture. All types gathered there. The owner was Claude James, a woman with the reputation of having personally tossed out several rowdy male customers. According to one friend, Claude's arm was as thick as his thigh. The few times I saw her she was pleasant but her reputation was such that I did not want to cross her.

One night we made the rounds from La Fonda to the Plaza to the Palace to Claude's. There I met Jim Morris, a friend of Hal's from the 1930s, a painter whom Hal had met in New York. Jim had studied at the Art Students League in New Yor and was one of two Santa Fe artists featured in a *Time* magazine story in the 1940s.

Jim's studio was within sight of Hal's, and Hal had pointed him out to me several times as Jim made his way up the road. He was short, Hal's height, slightly paunchy, with gray hair and mustache. This night he was drunk, swaying ever so slightly as he held onto the bar with both hands and talking with a thick tongue. Hal went up to Jim, who was looking the other way, and punched him on the arm. Jim lurched, turning his head at the same time, his eyes widening, saying, "Hal West you son of a bitch!" He stepped forward awkwardly and punched Hal on the arm. Hal laughed delightedly. Jim laughed and said, "You old son of a bitch, buy me a drink."

"Why hell no, you tight bastard, I've known you for twenty years and you've never bought me anything, not so much as a sody pop."

"What do you mean I never did?"

"Name one time."

"Well, if I didn't, it was because you're not worth it."

"I'll buy you a drink, Jim," I said. "What do you want?"

"Guiness."

"Don't waste your money, son," Hal said. "He won't be grateful."

"That's all right," I said.

Claude's raged thick with people. The jukebox blasted rock and roll. When Claude's closed, the three of us staggered arm-in-arm down the middle of Canyon Road, me in the middle.

"Let's go to my house for a toddy, son," Hal said to me, so off the three of us stumbled.

At the back door Hal leaned against the wall, swaying while he dug into his coat pockets for the key as I held him up and Jim soliloquized on something wild and detached. Inside we poured ourselves drinks. Finally I became so bleary eyed I went into the main room, took a cushion from a chair, threw it on the floor, lay down and passed out.

This was my introduction to Santa Fe nightlife.

*****

Why did I say that meeting Hal was the beginning of my life in America? After all, I had already experienced much of America. I had hitchhiked and ridden freights across country. I had lived for two months in a dying New Mexican village, had spent summers in rural Ohio, wandered Manhattan, attended a southern military academy and observed up close the upper-middle-class life of New Canaan.

So while I had experienced a scattering of American peoples and types by the time I met Hal, meeting Hal opened the flood-gates of experience. My education proceeded at a faster pace.

My reaction to Hal, I think, had much to do with his person-ality, which was distinctive, and came from an older America. It also had to do with the fact that Hal was very much a part of Santa Fe's Canyon Road art colony, and therefore very much a part of Santa Fe's larger culture. Here was the first vital regional culture I came to know. Looking back on it by several years I realized that Hal had been my key to that experience. He was the first man of solidly regional character with whom I bonded.

By the time I met Hal, I had decided to befriend distinctly American types. By this time I no longer thought about an American soul, whatever that was, but now searched for the American character.

Knowing Hal opened something inside of me, a freedom and ease among adults I had not experienced before. I was now thoroughly launched on my journey into what I hoped would be a discovery of America.

Santa Fe with its assortment of Indians, Hispanics and Anglos, gays and straights, alcoholics, artists, businessmen and ranchers, gave me an excellent measure by which to judge New Canaan. The culture of New Canaan, which is to say the culture of upper middle class America, was the first American culture I knew. It was to become—in less affluent versions—the culture of late twentieth century America.

TWO
New Canaan

I often return in my mind to New Canaan because New Canaan's values are stark indicators of much that went wrong in America. The striving for money and the respectability to be gained by it obliterated the sense of vocation and meaningful work that may have lain buried inside many of New Canaan's commuter families.

The loss of vocation and the abandonment of meaningful work clearly is a story that began long before New Canaan's founding. It is a story that goes back to colonial America. Between 1732 and 1758, when he published yearly editions of *Poor Richard's Almanac*, Benjamin Franklin encouraged his fellow citizens to practice frugality and to spare no effort in the acquisition of money and property. The almanacs were peppered with aphorisms, which Franklin chose because they "inculcated industry and frugality, as the means of promoting wealth, and thereby securing virtue . . . " Wealth, then, he identified with virtue and poverty with vice. Franklin's aphorisms were later excerpted from the almanacs and published as *The Way to Wealth*.

Invoking Franklin can help ease one's conscience and justify one's greed and desire for "getting on" and "making something of oneself." So, too, can the Calvinist belief that wealth is a sign of God's grace. Once one's conscience is eased, the heart's longing for vocation is smothered, unfelt, and easily denied.

Many years after I left New Canaan, Mother told me that Father had really wanted to teach. After graduating from Harvard Business School he had joined the faculty of the Tennessee Military Academy. He and Mother stayed there one or two years before they left for Pittsburgh, where Father went to work for U.S. Steel and began his life in corporate America. In later years he laughed at himself for having gone off the track.

Father's story is a common one. We Americans, and most people worldwide—thanks to American influence—have forgotten what it means to have a vocation. In the centuries before industrialization, men and women earned their bread through labor and craft. They were artisans and makers, and performed useful work, producing goods and services that people needed. Their work was honorable and satisfying and was necessary to maintaining their relatively simple economies.

In several of his books, Sherwood Anderson wrote about the transformation of American consciousness during his Ohio boyhood. The coming of machinery, Anderson wrote repeatedly, spurred that transformation. As farmers, for example, saw how much more land they could plant and harvest with the new machines, they hungered for more land and the money they could make with it.

As fewer farmers were needed on the land, they migrated to cities where people were needed to tend and repair machines. People were needed to package the goods the machines produced. More and more salesmen were needed to sell the machine-made products. Trades disappeared one by one as machines made them obsolete. Workers forgot their fathers' crafts, they forgot how to work skillfully with their hands. Their hearts were no longer in their work, nor were their minds. They became machine tenders.

Other men were needed to manage the machine tenders.

Then came the Great Depression in 1929. The men of my father's generation, many of whom had come off farms and had lived through the Depression, were determined never again to experience want.

Horatio Alger's absurdist novels about Dick the shoeblack or Sam the newsy who became millionaires fed their hunger and spirits. The shoeblack in the days of labor strife would never have been able to rise above a factory worker, as Alger knew.

Many of Alger's heroes did become rich, however, but only because some millionaire admired their grit and stick-to-it-tiveness, their courage or honesty and gave them a job. The Alger hero was not an entrepreneur. He did not build an industrial or business empire. But the myth of the Alger hero was reiterated time and again by my father, who had little use for my ambition to write and, I suppose, considered it a definite sign of a romantic who was unable or unwilling to face the hard facts of life.

A variant of the Alger myth was expressed in a book I found in my father's small collection—*The Man Nobody Knows,* by Bruce Barton. The man of the title is Jesus. In Barton's account, Jesus was a dynamic businessman who was ruthless with himself—he slept on the ground and traveled on foot—in creating what was to become the world's most influential corporation. Jesus, according to Barton, built his organization with twelve men "picked from the bottom ranks of business." Yet Jesus not only inspired his twelve initial associates, but growing crowds. Eventually, long after his death, his dynamic message was accepted by millions and spread across the globe.

I do not remember God ever mentioned in Barton's book. Perhaps God is mentioned, but Barton's emphasis has nothing to do with spirit or spirituality. It has everything to do with making a success out of oneself. *The Man Nobody Knows* is a book for go-getters and small town boosters. It was a national best seller in the 1920s and continues to sell to this day.

In retrospect I realize that the drive for riches and security that possessed the men of the upper middle-class communities of America in the 1950s and 1960s also obliterated whatever sense of vocation that may have lurked in their hearts.

The next two or three waves of New Canaan residents have had even less sense of something lost than earlier residents. Many years after I left New Canaan, I returned one weekday afternoon for a few hours to glimpse the surfaces. I saw a woman step out of her sports car wearing an exorbitantly expensive dress, looking as though she were headed for a cocktail party. Her children were with her, and I concluded that she was shopping. I noticed that all the cars surrounding hers were expensive, many were foreign.

This was what she and those like her had to drive and wear in order not to lose face. This is what her class believed in: this was what had value. A few minutes earlier I had visited the town library to speak to the director. She had written a glowing review of one of my books for a national journal, but I was told—by assistants who talked as though they were clerks at Tiffany's and I was delivering morning coffee— that she was in a meeting.

I suddenly felt ashamed of my own very decent clothes. I was totally out of my element. There was no question that these people, who lived on surfaces, had no respect for anything outside their culture.

This newer generation of materialists spent their money. This is what "keeping up with the Joneses" had come to. My parents' generation invested their money. A good house in a respected community, a membership in a golf club, an investment in their children's college education—these were pretty much the extent of their big expenditures. The men of my parents' generation did not earn the salaries that the later men did, nor did they collect stock options. The materialism of the upper middle-class of my parents' generation had degenerated into the hyper-materialism that continues to throttle America to this day.

New Canaan was the first culture and society that I knew intimately and became the base line from which I have been able to distinguish other cultures and societies.

***

For Father, wealth was a sign of virtue, proof that one had worked hard and persevered. I think for Father the greatest of all virtues were hard work and perseverance. Work not only secured wealth, but provided security and well being for the family. Honest dealing was a close second to work and perseverance. Beyond work, honest dealing, and perseverance there may not have existed other virtues.

I believe that most of the men in New Canaan and like towns thought as Father did. They may have been Catholic, or Episcopalian, or Methodist, or any other Protestant sect, but they were Americans and had inherited the Puritan—which is to say Calvinist— belief in wealth as proof of virtue. But for these men virtue was reduced to hard work, perseverance, and honest dealing.

Like the New Canaanites, early Calvinists worked hard but unlike New Canaanites their hard work was linked to their sense of vocation and duty to God. Lurking behind this may have been the idea that man as maker was imitating God the Maker, and therefore as a maker, man was godly. But with the growth of science and technology in the West came the gradual death of God, and so the Calvinist belief in work as a duty to God collapsed. For Europeans and Americans, nothing could possibly any longer connect virtue to God since God was dead.

Six decades after the materialists of the sixties have passed on, their successors, the hyper-materialists, have abandoned two of their predecessors' cardinal virtues. Perseverance remains, but financial speculation has replaced hard, useful work. For the speculators who amassed fortunes by collapsing the housing market and sending many thousands onto the streets, honest dealing is a positive impediment to success.

My revulsion with New Canaan with its emphasis on hardheadedness pushed me into other places. Books and imagination and dreaming had no place in New Canaan. And if hard work, perseverance and honest dealing were the only virtues, then imagination and inquiry and learning for the sake of knowing meant little or nothing. What power could imagination and the need to know have in the face of those who ran America, those who had no use for imagination or of knowing for the sake of knowing? What could a sonnet be worth? Of what value was a watercolor? What strength can a piece of paper splashed with color have against a

100-ton locomotive or the imponderable weight of a skyscraper? Imagination was dead before the force of action.

My strong desire to know about other ways of living pulled me elsewhere. My mind's lens saw much but judged little, not morally and certainly not in terms of whether he has money and is therefore is to be respected or he is poor and therefore of little worth. Neither dirt, nor primitive conditions, nor poverty repulsed me. Rather, driven by a desire to become a part of this life or that, I traveled. The early hitchhiking trips and sojourns of my youth showed me new ways of living, therefore ways I must learn and enter, new ways of being.

THREE
New Canaan (1960-61)

For young New Canaanites who were supposed to fit into a particular slot but did not—perhaps they refused to acknowledge the rules—there was psychiatry. Inattention at school was a behavior problem and clearly indicative of some deeper problem.

Sean Fitzpatrick became a friend in high school. I only knew him by sight in junior high, where he excelled in his classes. By his second year in high school, he stopped studying and was held back. Neither Sean nor I fit in. Our guidance counselor, whose job was to "adjust" the unadjusted, called our parents. Sessions with a Stamford psychiatrist were arranged. Since we were both ashamed of seeing this psychiatrist, neither knew the other was going. Only years later did we discover we had both gone. I went to two or three sessions. The psychiatrist, of course, kept silent for long stretches, then would ask what I was thinking. Once I told him, "I was wondering when you were going to ask me what I was thinking."

In the course of our discussions, searching for something to tell the psychiatrist and break the silence, I told him I was drawing portraits of classmates. What I did not tell him was that these were exaggerations modeled after Fritz Eichenburg's illustrations for Dostoevsky's novels. He wanted to see them. When I brought them, he was much interested. Now he was getting somewhere! The facial distortions obviously recorded something disturbed within me. He asked how I felt about these classmates. Pleased at being able to disappoint him, I happily told him the origin of the style. His response was, "Oh."

At the end of the second or third session I told him he should be talking to my parents, not me. That was the end of the visits. Mother was furious! How dare I accuse her and Father of being the source of my rebellion and disinterest in school?

My only escape from the rules and rigidity of New Canaan came from the McDonald brothers—and the friends who gathered at their home. The McDonald family did not conform to New Canaan standards. For one, the boys and their stepfather lacked the obsessive attention every New Canaanite was supposed to devote to his lawn. For another, the McDonald home, unlike other New Canaan homes, was lived in. Once, when the McDonald brothers, Eddy and Phil, visited our home, Eddy—looking about the living room—said, "There should be red ropes to keep people off the furniture."

The McDonald home was like none I had ever seen. To begin with, their dog was chained to the bottom of the staircase, four feet from the front door. As soon as you entered he leaped at you, not to bite or play, but to hump you. He would grasp your thigh and start pumping. Eddy or Phil would yell, "Get down, Morris!" and perhaps pull him off. The guest would stumble away asking, "Whatsa matter with that crazy dog?"

"Ah, he's horny," they would laugh and the visitor would make his way to a living room sofa or chair, wondering where to sit. The stuffed chairs and sofas were piled with magazines and newspapers. More newspapers were scattered across the floor and coffee table, which always had an ashtray piled with cigarette butts. The little sister's toys and games—stuffed dolls, crayons, and drawings—were strewn about.

Beyond the living room was the dining room, which no one probably ever used. The dining table was always loaded with a wild assortment of oddments—newspapers and paperbacks, perhaps an unused tea set, a hair dryer, or a martini shaker, and piles of comic books.

Mrs. McDonald had remarried a small rumpled man named Stevens. Off the dining room was a smaller room, their secret drinking quarters, though it was never a secret when they were drinking. Every evening I visited they would be sitting in chairs around a battered table littered with an ashtray, half-smoked packs of cigarettes, crumpled Kleenex and dog-eared books. They would have a bottle of bourbon and try to kill it before the night was over. Their conversations usually began quietly, as though they did not want the boys to hear. (We would be in the living room, perhaps recording improvised skits). But as the evening progressed Mr. and Mrs. Stevens would get drunk and their voices get louder and we could hear them distinctly.

"Jack! I told you that was not right!"

"Well, who gives a goddamn if it's right, I just want to get the job done."

"Why, for God's sake"--- spitting this out--- "can't you do something right for once!"

And that was only the beginning; by eleven o'clock they would be screaming at each other. At first I was shocked and tried to listen, but as years went on it became so boring I just tuned it out as everyone else did. At least none of us ever talked about it.

Naturally I felt more comfortable at the McDonald house than at my own or at any other New Canaan home. Sean Fitzpatrick, I'm sure, felt as I did. Anything went at the McDonald house. At our annual Christmas gathering there, someone would inevitably be shoved into the Christmas tree. As Mrs. Stevens heard yells and laughter coming from the living room, she knew what was about to happen and would shout, "No! Leave the tree alone!" We paid no attention, and someone would be shoved onto the tree and go crashing down amid a shattering of bulbs.

In sensibility, thought, and appearance Eddy and Phil and our mutual friend, Larry Blake, were far from the mass of New Canaan students, who wore nicely pressed cloths, had neatly trimmed hair, and smiled. These were obedient children. These were what Mother called "nice" young people. It was inevitable that the girls in this mass of "nice" adolescents would marry boys like those in New Canaan high school, boys who would grow into model executives with plush jobs and homes in towns like New Canaan, or Darien, or Greenwich. Naturally I did not spend time with them, but with Eddy, Phil and Larry.

Eddy was fat with close-cut hair, a snub nose and colorless plastic eyeglass frames. He lived at home in a tower off one corner of the house. Larry, his best friend, had once been invited upstairs to Eddy's garret. The room was a chaos of litter—*Playboy* magazines, crumpled comic books, paperbacks, and newspaper clippings strewn throughout, even on the unmade bed. The ceiling and walls were plastered over with *Playboy* centerfolds. Larry said it was worse than any other room in the house, which would have earned it a record of some sort.

Eddy wrote a weekly sports column for the local newspaper and managed a track team. I later discovered that although he did not have a high school diploma, Eddy had gotten such good recommendations from our vice principal that he was admitted to Antioch College, but had dropped out. Eddy was said to be one of the brightest guys in school.

Larry was also highly gifted. Eddy and Larry were a year older than Phil and I, and spent hours improvising and tape recording comedic sketches in send ups of ads and news stories.

On my first evening at their home, Phil played some of Eddy and Larry's improvisations. Phil and I began recording our own, but in all the years I knew the McDonalds I could never match Eddy or Larry's wit, or their ability to mimic the sounds of America's many tongues. The recordings and the gags continued for nine years, from 1961 through the summer of 1968, after I graduated from college.

The McDonalds and I were fans of W.C. Fields and had seen his short film, *The Golf Specialist*, in which Fields (who loved golf) has one mishap after another on the course and cheats when he can. Since golf was a huge New Canaan pastime, and since I considered it idiotic, Eddy and I conceived the idea of making our own golf film, which Eddy titled, *Golf Au Go-Go*. Go-go dancers— scantily dressed women shaking their cans to garish music—were then popular bar entertainment.

The film centered on my golfing misadventures. We began shooting it at my parents' country club. There, in a snit at having shot several balls into a pond, I threw my iron in the water. A party of golfers saw this and we hurriedly moved to another hole. From there I shot a ball to the edge of the course. The rest of the film followed me as I kept shooting the ball further and further from the country club. At one point I hit a seven-iron shot down a residential sidewalk near New Canaan's business district, and then putted through Breslow Brothers variety store. "Golf!? In Breslows?" said one of the brothers in his Yiddish accent, and let us do it.

Practical jokes were the breath of life to us. Norman Cousins, a famous liberal writer and publisher of *The Saturday Review,* lived down the road from us. Eddy came by one day with a road sign that read, "Keep right," that he and Phil had managed to uproot somewhere and said we were going to plant it at the entrance to Cousins' drive. We propped it again his stonewall.

A few years after high school, when I returned home for vacations, I spent most of my time with Eddy and Phil and the gang, Mother said, "I lost you when you began seeing the McDonalds."

My sister, meanwhile, was fitting in with the "normal" kids. Many years later she told me she conformed because she saw how I, four years her senior, was treated for my independence. I never had Father's approval. I did not share his values; I would not become a businessman, as he wanted. For all of his life, up until a few years before he died, he resented my steadfast independence.

"Oh, Bob," my mother once said, "Why don't you have some nice friends, like Mark Ballard." Mark Ballard was a nondescript boy, well adjusted to New Canaan life. The thing was always to have nice friends, those who conformed to expectations. Conforming to expectations indicated that a youngster would succeed. It indicated that the child was grateful for the choices his parents had made, and that their choices would be his. I was not making the choices my parents made: I did not want "nice" friends: I did not study: I did not want their life.

I had to create my own. When at home I read, or painted, or listened to jazz and classical music. Not only did the arts stimulate my imagination and feed my emotions, they enabled me to escape for an hour or two from the dull and brutal world of Calvin's heirs. In Father's mind, I'm sure, these interests marked me as unfit for the struggle of life.

Imagine then what he must have thought of my friends. My parents had seen the McDonald house near the business district. We had driven by it and they must have known immediately that the McDonalds did not belong in their social circle, that no one who came from a home with a crazy Gothic tower surrounded by untrimmed bushes eight feet tall and an unmowed lawn could share their values. When my parents saw the house, Father began asking questions about the McDonalds. What does their father do?

"Well, their father is dead. Mrs. McDonald is now married to Mr. Stevens. He edits a magazine."

He edited something akin to a catalog but I thought "magazine" gave him greater respectability. I had to defend my friends, which meant defending the stepfather. That defense probably meant little, since in Father's mind Eddy, Phil, and I all fit into the slot marked "maladjusted."

FOUR
Breaking Out (summer 1961)

The summer of my seventeenth year was the summer everything came to a head. I was repeating biology in summer school. At home I spent hours imagining myself hitchhiking west, looking at the red, blue, and yellow lines on oil company maps, tracing out my route, thinking of cars barreling down two-lane country highways and of trucks roaring over expressways. I had read Carl Sandburg's autobiography, *Always the Young Strangers* and Burl Ives' memoir. Both men had ridden the rails and lived with hobos. I read Dos Passos *U.S.A.* and was fascinated by the story of Mac, the printer, who rode freights across country. I, too, want to jump freights.

I wanted to work on combine crews harvesting wheat on the Great Plains from Texas to Alberta. I pictured the great combines in endless wheat fields. I saw great stacks of clouds above the plains and cattle herds and cowboys on horseback. I wanted to see the ore boats in Duluth, cotton pickers in the Delta, Navajos in Monument Valley herding sheep. I had seen pictures of the rows of smokestacks on the Chicago-Gary skyline, buttes and twisted rocks of the Arizona desert, the piers of the Seattle harbor. I wanted to see all the iconic places and workers of America the myth.

When I asked my parents if I could hitchhike to my grandparents' home in Defiance, Ohio my mother was terrified.

"Oh, no, son," she said, "That's not for you. You're too high class for that."

"Lots of American writers did it," I told her.

But she insisted, "You're too high class for that."

When I broached the idea to Father, he shook his head and said, "I can't allow it. It's too dangerous hitching that long a distance. If you take a bus to Toledo, I'll let you hitchhike to Defiance."

"That's only twenty-four miles," I complained. "That's not worth it."

Later that summer, as I kept insisting on my trip, my mother told me a story she had heard in her bridge group. "Mark Ballard was hitchhiking on Route 7 and got picked up by a truck driver who made advances. Mark told the man to stop the truck and let him out, but he kept driving, and Mark had to jump from the moving truck." My mother fixed me with a stare. "There's only one reason a man would want to hitchhike."

I became furious. "I'm not like that!" I yelled. It never occurred to me that she was, in this odd way, trying to protect me.

By the end of summer school I knew my biology grade was a C, at best. I did not want to face Father, who would be furious for days. On the Saturday my grade was due to arrive in the mail, my parents told me to cut the lawn, and left to play golf. As soon as they drove off I stuffed my backpack with a sleeping bag and clothes and called Sean Fitzpatrick. I told him I was hitchhiking to Ohio and to come over. Sean waited as I cut the huge lawn and later as I wrote my parents a note, telling them my plan.

Sean drove me downtown to the train station. I boarded the train and waved goodbye from a window and turned to face the distant city as the carriage rolled and bounced over rails.

At Stamford I transferred to the main line, racketing through town after town—Old Greenwich, Greenwich, Waterbury, Rye. At last the train clacked over rails to Harlem, where it sat briefly atop the city at the 125th Street station before resuming its plunge into downtown through an unimaginably long tunnel lit by sidelights that illuminated occasional tracks converging, paralleling, or crossing one another. We kept rattling on to Grand Central Station, to a long cement platform with a crash of steam, hisssssssss!!!!!!!

"Graaannnd Cennntrallll!" the conductor bawled. I had been gripping the straps of my backpack ever since we first went underground and now walked to the door and stepped on the platform to smells of oil and steam and walked into the great hall with imperial arched ceiling and out into the roaring city.

I walked across traffic-filled streets and along the tumult of sidewalks to the Lincoln Tunnel. I tried walking through but a guard waved me off. I stood beside the road on a great curve where the traffic roared as cars careened on their lunge for the tube. I breathed lungfulls of heavy fumes. Car after car flew by on the exodus to New Jersey. Finally, the traffic thinned and a red Volkswagen pulled over. I ran and got in, my excitement great as the driver threw the car into gear.

His radio was airing the World Series. This was the year everyone followed the great Yankee hitter, Roger Maris. That day he was hitting home runs and the crowd was on its feet. Here was another Ruth! The driver and I talked all the way through the tunnel about Maris, the games, and my trip. We shot onto the Jersey shore across the Pulaski Skyway to a vision of railyards and stacks of industrial goods piled outside warehouses, of trains and massive factories pouring smoke into the great skyweb.

Across the skyway I got a ride at an entrance to Route 22, a highway that ran across Pennsylvania. An hour later, outside Allentown, just across the line from New Jersey, I called home collect.

"Yes," my father said, "I'll accept the changes . . . Bob! Where are you?"

"Allentown, Pennsylvania. On Route 22."

"Thank goodness you're okay."

"Yeah, I'm fine."

"Where are you staying tonight?"

"I'll probably throw out my sleeping bag somewhere near here."

"All right, be careful. I'll call grandmother and grandfather to tell them you're coming by bus to Toledo and hitchhiking from there."

By nightfall I was eating a hamburger, fries, pumpkin pie and drinking a malt at a roadside restaurant. By the time I got around to the pie I was so full I nearly choked. I walked slowly back to the road, waiting until the nausea subsided. The sky was dark, headlights raced past. I did not think I would get a ride. I thought perhaps I should climb the fence behind the restaurant and spread my sleeping bag on the field, but decided to try hitching for half an hour. I crooked a thumb, and within minutes I heard a screech of brakes and whirled to see two red taillights swerve under a bridge abutment. I expected to hear the crash of metal, but the taillights stopped just before the underpass. I watched, wondering if it had stopped for me, then ran. As I approached, a man got out and told me to get in. When he climbed in after me and slammed the door, I smelled alcohol. I wished I could get out.

The one who had stepped out put his arm on the seat in back of me. I tensed, thinking he would grab my neck. The driver was smaller than I, but the other man was big. I thought they would stop the car and drag me outside. Miles passed, I waited. The big man picked beers out of a bag at his feet, gave one to the driver and offered me one. I had never tasted beer before, but not wanting to seem afraid, I tasted it. It was bitter. I forced the first mouthfuls down, but by the time I finished the can I was no longer afraid of the men, and was talking freely.

They were truckers who had bought a chicken farm in West Virginia and were headed there. They gave me another beer. I became one of them, a man of the road, doing what I had dreamed of doing all summer, with more adventures waiting in the next state. They stopped for a pisscall and a tank of gas, and the men switched places. I got a closer look at the big man, who was dressed in green chinos and an oil-stained shirt.

Somewhere on a backcountry road, as they searched for a southern route into West Virginia, we stopped at a diner. I followed them inside, lurching and weaving after them, proud to be with them, thinking myself a hero of the American Night. We stood at the counter where the driver ordered piles of hotdogs with sauer-kraut, relish, onions, and mustard. While we waited, he pulled a creased and oil-stained map from his back pocket, unfolded it and laid it on the counter. He was looking for a route to Union, West Virginia.

I thought that for truckers they were ignorant of the roads, and I argued with the driver about the quickest route, hoping they were drunk enough to bring me closer to my destination. The driver, a barrel-chested, black-haired wild man, drunk, thumped his forefinger heavily onto the map, insisting on his route while I drunkenly, cunningly, tried to point out that their quickest route was really further north. When the order came we hustled back to the car and roared off, with what I thought was the best food I had had in years.

Somewhere further on in the night they stopped at a cross-roads, looking at road signs, trying to make out which way to go. Later, when I was sleeping on the back seat amid oily rags, they picked up a hitchhiker who chewed a big wad of gum and wore a red baseball cap. He told them his story. He had been bumming off his sister and brother-in-law but they had thrown him out and now he cursed them. When they careened around curves he leaned on me. The driver—the same wild-haired man as before—was taking the car around a narrow two-lane highway at 80 m.p.h. By then the beer had worn off and I was expecting us to go hurtling into the woods, upside-down, the side of the car bashed in, wheels spinning, groans from inside.

I was awake well before dawn when they let the bum off at a town. I looked at my map to see where I should leave them and hitchhike north. When they left me off, I wished them luck with their chicken farm and the big man gave the other a knowing look. Had the chicken farm been a yarn?

I stayed the next month in Defiance with my grandparents. I spent mornings with Grandfather on the farm, helping him weed his vegetable garden and picking strawberries, blueberries, and raspberries. Afternoons I sometimes walked to the town library and read. The library was on the high grounds above the Miami River next to the grounds of old Fort Defiance, whose outline was now marked by long mounds. The fort stood above the confluence of the Maumee and Miami Rivers, where river traffic could be seen a long ways off. Sometimes I walked the perimeter of the fort, imagining the stockade and cannons, seeing howling Indians leaping over rocks and bushes and soldiers firing long rifles, the smoke of the rifles lazying upwards.

In a month I took a bus back home. I was headed for prep school that fall and had assignments to prepare.

FIVE
New York State (1962-63)

Bentley Academy was located ninety miles north of New York City. It was a small school of ninety students, set in the foothills of the Taconics, a rolling land of dairy farms and woods.

My one year at Bentley, my senior year, was the first consciously happy year of my life. This was the year I grew out of my protective shell and laughed. In New Canaan I had been unsure of myself, had few friends, and barely talked to girls. At Bentley my inhibitions dropped away.

My first night at Bentley I went to a party for seniors at the headmaster's house. When I entered the kitchen for a cup of coffee, I saw a girl standing apart from the others. Hers was a beautiful soft Irish face framed with long chestnut tresses, which she twisted wistfully between her fingers. I wanted to know her, very much, but she looked far more mature than I. She was probably a returning student and I was a newcomer. I was drawn to her. I wanted to know her, but I was nervous. At last I introduced myself. Her name was Deborah Clemens.

We spoke only occasionally during the next six months, but when we did talk and began to know one another, a lasting friendship was seeded.

***

Father sent me to Bentley hoping my grades would improve and I would be accepted into an Ivy League college. Surely he knew that home life had affected my grades, but did he know how much New Canaan High School had also affected them? Except for art classes, there was nothing about that school to like. The students were cliquish, with the rich kids at the top of the social pyramid. Their clothes were always spanking new and their hair well trimmed. The boys wore button down Oxford shirts and polished loafers. The girls wore white blouses with rounded collars, buttoned at the top. When these boys and girls grew up, you knew they would marry into their own class. They were carbon copies of their parents.

I disliked Dick and Jane, as I now think of these manikin-like teens, but I feared the hoods. Every year I had a fight with at least one of them. I became their target probably because I was skinny and quiet, a seemingly easy mark.

The hoods were an odd assortment of body types and ethnic groups, but they had two things in common—they were townies with low self-esteem and they were not very bright. There were about five of them, I think. There was the skinny Irish kid, Reilly, and the skinny, very ugly Italian kid, Abbate. The only other one I remember by name was Ken Jones, their leader, the only muscular one in the group.

Reilly challenged me to a fight in seventh grade on school grounds, and I think the fight ended with one punch to Reilly's face. In ninth grade Abbate challenged me and we went off grounds to settle it. We faced each other more than a dozen feet apart and I ran at him yelling and knocked him down.

Still, I was always fearful of a rematch, or a challenge from Jones, who came at me the next year and slammed a rock hard fist into my shoulder. I eased away and into my school bus. The threat from Jones ended when the football team made it clear to him that if he hurt me, they would hurt him.

At Bentley, unlike New Canaan, adults and adolescents did not measure one another. There were no cliques. Our teachers became friends. Not surprisingly, surrounded by friendly schoolmates in a small school in beautiful countryside, and with caring teachers, my grades improved. Life was good. I painted a mural on the basement wall of the art studio; I helped cut a cross-country ski trail; I skied and played hockey; I played piano in a jazz trio. Life was, indeed, good.

Life at Bentley was active, with much of it lived out of doors. Boys walked up and down a long hill three times a day for meals, and boys and girls spent afternoons playing sports or working grounds crew. That's where I met Rick Graham, on grounds crew.

Rick, who was a year younger than I, became a pal. Rick was short and curly-haired with a voice that boomed when it was not cracking. He rushed everywhere and talked and laughed loudly. His exuberance was infectious. He would come up behind me, slap me on the back and yell, "How ya doing, Wolfie boy?" I had never before known anyone like him. Rick lived by impulse and listened to rules when it suited him. Had Rick and I not chummed together, I would have lived that year by the rules and not have lost so much of my protective shell.

Each afternoon Rick and I reported to the maintenance shop for our assignment. The shop housed the school's trucks, lawn mowers, tractors, hand-tools, and other equipment. Rick and I worked together.

Some days we were assigned to collect the garbage from school buildings. We would jump in a pickup and tear off. Rick usually drove, bouncing us over dirt roads. When we came to a cluster of cans he would brake with a jerk and at the same time leap out and slam the door, grab a can and dump it in back. We made pickups at nine buildings, ending with the kitchen where we emptied huge slop barrels and hosed their insides clean before swabbing them with brooms. Afterwards we would ply the cook for juice and cookies, and lounge for an hour before dumping the garbage in a field a mile inside the woods.

Sometimes we stayed at the kitchen so long that the shop would send Millard, one of the grounds men, after us. He usually found us with our feet on a dining table and the work undone. He would yell at us until we shuffled to our feet and followed him outside where he would supervise us as we finished the job, usually pitching in vigorously and getting it done faster than we could. We, however, thought the old man could not get work elsewhere, and spoke sarcastically to him. Brenda, the school cook, told us once when Millard was outside, "Don't you make fun of that old man, he's good," and we never mocked him again.

***

For the year at Bentley I dreamed of America, its work and people and the land stretching incredible distances west, south and north. My dream was to tramp the country, walk southern swamps; live in snow-covered Canadian woods; work the fishing boats off Texas and Louisiana shores, hauling in huge nets full of shrimp; work the oil rigs of Oklahoma; ride freight trains cross country at midnight under the stars; herd cattle in Montana; live with the Navajo in Monument Valley.

I knew stockbrokers, advertising copywriters, and managers of American corporations; I wanted nothing to do with ticker tapes and stock quotations, with the slam of New York traffic, with the hustle of business, running across a midtown Manhattan plaza to an office, to grimly carry a briefcase on a plane to San Francisco. I wanted the life of a trapeze artist swinging across open space, body arched, arms outstretched for partner with feet hooked onto bar swinging towards me. I wanted to be on a flat car on a freight rushing across the Texas Panhandle or Nebraska cornfields. I wanted to play jazz trumpet, blasting out golden notes solid and well hit, filling the room with sounds mad enough to drive the listeners out of their seats and shouting.

I wanted to ride on surfboards under curling waves shooting fast to the shore; to sail a yawl or sloop far out in the Pacific; to read the quadrant or sextant and know my way anywhere under a night sky; to camp in forests for months by myself and feel at home; to run long foot races leaving everyone in the dust and the crowds roaring.

America was endless. Time did not exist. I would never grow old. America was a giant of the morning, a land of inestimable beauty that I would someday paint in murals and set down in novels. America offered endless adventure and I was in New York dairy country, a beautiful idyll of farms and pasture land. . . bidding my time.

I talked about America and last summer's hitchhike. Two students, who wrote their impressions of each student on note cards, said of me: "Likes Graham, loves America."

***

That March seniors took a bus to see a play at the Stockbridge School, nearby in Massachusetts. Deborah Clemens was the last to come aboard, enveloped in a huge raccoon coat. I sat alone, caught her eye and signaled her to sit with me. We began talking, and soon she was talking nonstop.

"What does your father do?" I asked. It was a question middle-class children were trained to ask.

"He committed suicide when I was three."

I could say nothing.

"He wrote some letters and poems that I still have. I don't know much about him. He was schizophrenic."

Her openness stunned me.

"My mother raised me several years before she married my stepfather. They have an apartment in New York and a home in Connecticut, near here. That's how I started at Bentley so many years ago, when it was an elementary school. I started here in fifth grade. I've been here longer than anyone else."

The bus rolled on. We talked on, and when I would start speaking she would interrupt; it reminded her of something and off she would go.

I was smitten. She was beautiful. Her eyes shined with an inner life. I wanted to see through those eyes.

I wanted to hold her hand; my own became sweaty. We both looked straight ahead. I agonized. Don't take too long, move now, hold out your hand. But the fear—perhaps she won't hold it— will draw away— embarrassment. Still not looking at her I lifted my hand and put it onto hers. She did not move, did not look at me, did not pull away. My fingers slid under hers, palm against palm. She accepted, her hand against mine. Our fingers found each other, interlocked, clasped.

We still do not look at each other. Acceptance is nonverbal. Warmth surges through my body. My heart beats fast, my throat tightens. I do not know what to say. Time passes, we say nothing, still do not look at each other, but ahead. I am fumbling in my mind for what to say.

"Where will you go next year?"

"Bennington, maybe."

"What do you want to do?"

"Dance."

"Did you grow up in New York?"

"Yes."

"I want to live there someday."

I saw myself on the top floor of a brownstone walkup. It was furnished with antique furniture, chairs with round carved backs, upholstered in velvet. I was a writer. New York was the chic world of Holly Golightly . . . the world of Tiffany's and jewels . . . museums . . . the precision of Salvador Dali . . . sharp, well dressed ladies in heels and black suits. It was the world of cracking flags and sharp, yellow taxis cutting to a stop . . . of diner at the Plaza Hotel . . . Scribners & Sons bookstore with the broad staircase to the upper balcony. It was diner at the Fulton Fish Market . . . prowling used bookstores on Fourth Avenue . . . sitting on a bench in Washington Square by the arch. I was a writer. Writing what? I did not know. It would be years before I did much writing. It was a dream.

***

Warm winds returned. . . snow melted into rivulets. . . life stirred in the woods.

Sometime in May Rick clomped into my room, sat on my desk and announced, "We're hitchhiking to Ashley Falls."

"But Rick, it's illegal."

That winter Rick and I had hitchhiked to a nearby town in defiance of the rules and trudged back at night four miles through snow across fields and over a hill.

"Save the excuses, pal, let's get moving," he said in a mock tough-guy voice. And then, in his high-pitched, cracking voice said, "They ain't gonna catch us. Come on."

Knowing I would follow him, Rick swung off the desk and stomped outside.

One ride came from a slow moving pickup driven by a farmer who asked if I wanted a job. In between rides Rick and I stood alongside the road, shoving one another, talking in goofy voices. At one point we stood across from a pasture of thick grass with a wide stream cutting through. Beyond the pasture were hills. Next to us was a power line.

"I'm gonna have a look-see," Rick said, and ambled over and began climbing the pole. "Can't see nothin'," he said from on high.

I scrambled up after him, thirty feet in the air, surveying the land. The road disappeared into the woods. We scrambled down and I looked at my sticky palms covered with gray paint. I looked back at the tower, wiped the paint off on leaves, and gave Rick a shove.

We walked up the road to a store where we bought luncheon meat, bread, and mustard. We followed the bank of a river, then jumped to a rock in the middle of the rushing water. There we sat and made sandwiches and ate. Afterwards we followed a dirt road into pine-covered hills, then left the road and scrambled up a hill towards the falls. As the hill became steeper we had to clamber over rocks until we faced a vertical rock cliff. We pulled ourselves up sheer precipices with only narrow handholds to grasp, our feet on a narrow ledge below.

When we stood atop the highest rock on the falls, the green hills sloped from all sides into a bowl. Behind us the hills arched higher and the river ran splashing down into pools, then twisted, forked, and swirled in pockets until it fell sixty feet, sparkling in the air before reaching the tranquil turquoise pool at the base.

From there it dropped further, slowly, then rapidly down into the valley beyond.

***

After graduation I lost touch with all my schoolmates, except Deborah. Only years later did I see Rick again, when I happened to be teaching at Bentley and tracked him down. Bentley was by then a dumping ground for troubled children whose parents did not want them.

Rick and another Bentley student, whose mother ran a prominent Madison Avenue art gallery, had volunteered for the Army in the buddy system and shipped off for Vietnam. Now they were running an electric repair company and living in New York State not far from Bentley. The Vietnam War had ended thirty years earlier and this was a different Rick—quieter and contained.

We were both married when my wife and I visited him at his home. We talked of Bentley and the people we had known, and then, wanting to be funny, I foolishly blurted, "You and Adam volunteered for Vietnam in the buddy system, thinking it was a good deal." I did not realize that with that remark I had destroyed the possibility of renewing our friendship. Only someone who has not been to war could make light of it.

I had broken a few rules before I met Rick, but all as a matter of defiance, and in reaction to something I did not like. With Rick it was different. I learned that you must break the rules once in awhile, or life narrows into routine and the ruts you travel deepen. Your sensibilities flatten out and you can no longer stumble upon the wonderful accidentals of life.

SIX
Omaha (summer 1963)

I was three days on the road and fourteen miles from Omaha on a clear stretch of Iowa highway surrounded by hay fields and the sky wide and blue with jagged clouds. I stood where the highway divided—one road headed west for Omaha and the other headed north. I had waited two hours and was becoming impatient when a salesman gave me a lift clear into Nebraska on the straightaway that raced into Omaha. On the outskirts of the business district we crossed a bridge above train tracks and I asked to be let off. I was sick of thumbing for rides and wanted to catch a freight to Denver or San Francisco.

I had worked earlier that summer after graduation on a survey crew, long enough to save money and go on the road. I had hitch-hiked from New York to Omaha and now wanted to hop a freight west.

I slung my pack over my shoulder and walked along a wide street between warehouses. A line of boxcars sat on a track in the middle of the street. At the end of the street I scrambled down an embankment to the tracks.

Long chains of freight cars lined the tracks. I knew nothing about hopping freights and became worried when I saw railroaders standing alongside cars. Or were they yard cops? I scrambled back up the embankment to the street with warehouses. An old man sat on steps in front of one of them.

"Say," I asked him, "can you tell me where I can catch a freight heading west?"

The old man did not turn around. I asked again. He looked at the street in front of him and said, "Nope."

I crossed into another street with warehouses. A fat security cop stood in a garage. He stepped out of the shadows with his hands on his hips and coughed.

I passed between parked trucks and climbed another embankment on top of which sat a depot and other railroad buildings. I walked to the depot and waited. A Union Pacific freight train sat on nearby tracks with several engineers standing around the cab. I wanted to ask where that freight was headed. Soon a young baggage handler on a motorized cart drove out of the depot. I walked up and asked him where I could catch a freight headed west. He said that the nearby Union Pacific train was headed west.

"Won't I get caught walking across the tracks to catch it?" I asked.

I was carrying a pack and the depot was crawling with people.

"Nah. The engineers don't care," he said.

He asked a lot of questions about where I had been and where I was headed.

"I admire someone your age free and on the road," he said and took off on the cart.

I did not want to chance walking across the tracks to talk to the engineers. Instead, I walked behind the depot and under a bridge when I spotted man in worn jeans, whom I took to be an engineer. When I called to him I saw he was old with a grizzled face and wore a red flannel shirt rolled up at the sleeves.

"Do you know anything about the trains heading west?" I asked.

"Where do you want to go? Denver?" His speech as thick and halting and his eyes were bloodshot.

"Yeah, Denver," I said. I did not care where I went, as long as it was west.

"Wel-l-l, you wanna ca-catch the spur to Lincoln an' then ca-catch the-the freight to Denver, makes no stops. Or you can hitch to Lincoln and catch the freight th-there."

"Nah," I said. "I don't wanna hitch. Sick of hitching."

"I-its only an hour to Lincoln on the-the road. Take Highway 90."

I was proud the way this fellow took me for a kid on the bum, though I was that only in a manner of speaking since I would soon be in college and had no worries about money or lodging.

"I'll take the freight. Tell me where to catch it."

"Under the bridge a ways down. As-ask a switchman. He'll tell you."

"When do I know I've reached Lincoln?"

I worried about that. I did not know if Lincoln was big or small. I wondered if there would be a sign for "Lincoln" at the depot. What if the Lincoln yard was an isolated, small stop on the prairie? And what if I got there and missed my connection to Denver? I did not want to spend the night sleeping on the cold prairie.

"You'll know. I'm going to Denver for the winter, gets too

cold here," he said.

I thanked him and walked along the tracks until I came to a shack where a switchman was eating supper. I wanted to make sure what the bum told me was right. I walked over and asked, "Where do I catch the spur to Lincoln?"

"They're making it up now. Over there." He pointed vaguely to his right. "Catch it under the third bridge from this one in about a half hour. It slows down there."

"How fast will it be going?"

"Bout fifteen miles an hour."

"Thanks."

I jogged along the tracks towards the third bridge. There was a bluff to my left. A train on top was pulling out.

"Maybe I should take that train," I thought. "Maybe it's heading west."

I was becoming nervous, thinking I would not catch the Lincoln spur. Immediately I saw another freight switch onto a nearby track. Thinking it was the Lincoln spur I ran to catch it. The engineer in the cab saw me and I wondered what he was thinking. It pulled out too fast for me and I lost it.

"Anyway," I thought, "it probably wasn't mine."

I saw another depot and crossed a line of tracks towards it. A railroader was walking towards me. I asked him the same questions I had asked the man in the shack, "Where do I catch the Lincoln spur?" He told me to wait at the same spot.

I jogged until I came to the bridge where I took off my pack. A line of five cars sat on the middle track and a long chain on the furthest track. I climbed up the side of a car and stood on the coupling, trying to figure how I would hold onto a car. It was going to be too dangerous hanging on with my arms and legs spread -eagled, holding onto the grab irons of two cars. I just hoped I could get a gondola or boxcar.

I looked to see if anyone was near. I sat on a track waiting for my train. I waited an hour and nothing came by. I was waiting there in the middle of this lonely country for a train to take me to another town just like this one. What was I to do there? Catch a freight to a city just as big and lonely? I wished I had never come on this trip.

The sun was going down and the smoke from Omaha's industry was just like the smoke back in Pittsburgh, or Chicago, or Allentown. I sat and waited.

It was getting dark. I heard sounds from a nearby factory and cars on the streets above the bluffs. The sun was gone and the lights from the factory and the bridge switched on. I wondered how to get out of Omaha and where to go. Back home. I climbed the embankment, which was littered with scraps of cardboard and broken bottles and rusted cans, and walked away from the freight yards, which offered nothing but a stretch of track and boxcars and clumps of grass blown in the gusty air. I walked into downtown Omaha through a residential section where people sat on rockers outside their homes in the cool night and I very much wanted to go home.

***

But where was home? Where was I headed? Not back to New Canaan or any town like it, nor to any job such as a man had to work to afford to live in a town like New Canaan. But if home was not to be in New Canaan, then where?

New York City drew me, but so did the farm country of the Middle West. The magnet of the Far West, especially Arizona, pictures of which I had studied in magazines, had an even stronger pull. San Francisco, where Kerouac and Ginsberg had lived—and perhaps still lived—drew me also. Many other boys my age were on the road, all of us searching.

And while I wandered the freight yards of Omaha, Sean Fitzpatrick was hitchhiking to San Francisco. Masses of us who came from the same background had rejected it. Where did anyone my age belong?

In just a few years a movement would coalesce; thousands of young people would leave their suburban homes for California, Vermont and New Mexico, looking for a simpler life. The hippies who established intentional communes wanted to find their roots in the soil. If their parents were competitive and materialistic, they must be cooperative and non-materialistic. Long live communal kitchens! Communal gardens! Communal dairy barns!

If the bourgeoisie's doors of perception were firmly bolted, they must be shattered! Altered consciousness would lead to a new world.

Since their parents believed in hierarchy, the hippies would be non-hierarchical. Decisions would be made by consensus.

These were the genuine idealistic hippies who wanted to create an alternative to the impersonal world that had taken hold in America. They wanted to live within a large family and tread lightly on the land.

But many, perhaps most, did not care. The communards came and went. One estimate says that most communards stayed on average only six months. Many who came, came for the free food, sex, and drugs. By the end of the Vietnam war, most of the communes dissolved and most of the hippies were reabsorbed into the machine from which they came.

In the conclusion to his 1962 book, *Literature and Western Man,* British author J.B. Priestley predicted that if we did not destroy ourselves in "one final idiot war" that we would find ourselves "hurrying in another direction," towards a loss of personality, or in his words, "we would soon cease to be a society composed of persons."

Intuitively perhaps that is what many of us young felt. To aspire to nothing more than a comfortable material life meant that nothing inside would be nurtured. That one's inmost self, whatever that was, would be suffocated. Surely the sincere communards sensed this but had no cultural foundation on which to build an alternative society.

Time has proven Priestley's prediction true. The American types, the iconic Americans of whom I went in search and found, have nearly all vanished. The men and women whom I found vital and alive, who lived by their own lights, are seldom visible today.

SEVEN
St. John's College (1963-64)

I was too young for college, especially one as intellectually demanding as St. John's in Annapolis. When St. John's non-elective
curriculum was redesigned in 1937, it became the country's first
great books college. I would have flourished in an art school or
experimental college, but not at a demanding liberal arts college.
I was certainly not prepared to dig deeply into Plato or Aristotle—and the freshman curriculum at St. John's included weeks of
readings from Plato and Aristotle.

That year I read very little of the assigned readings. I stopped
studying Greek and stopped studying the works of Euclid and
Ptolemy, which were the subjects of the freshman math tutorial.
I did not intentionally abandon the books; I came down with a
nasty case of athlete's foot. My foot swelled and by the time I
saw the college physician, it was infected. The infection spread to
my ankle and the lower part of the leg. I was sent to the infirmary
where I lay on my back in bed for a week with my foot raised. I
did not have my books and no one sent my assignments. I never
recovered from that lost week. I tried for a time to catch up with
the lessons, but it was an impossible task.

I suppose that at eighteen I believed that knowledge of the
great books would lead to profound understanding. The philosopher or wise man—I had not disentangled the two—were one
ideal of the human; the ascetic was another. Back in high school
my best friend, Sean Fitzpatrick, and I had pondered the ideals of
the warrior, the monk, the philosopher. We yearned to burn off the
dross within us and embrace an ideal. We talked about monks and
ascetic monastic orders like the Trappists.

We had read some of Thomas Merton's works, with his description of the Trappist vow of silence, daily devotions, work and
simple fare. I wanted to observe this life and wrote to the guest
master of St. Joseph's Abbey, a Trappist monastery in Spencer,
Massachusetts, asking if I could visit during winter break. Yes, he
replied, and after coming home to Connecticut, I drove one of our
cars to St. Joseph's and stayed four days.

I had several discussions with the guest master. I asked if he believed in the soul. I was not sure if I did.

"If I didn't believe we had a soul," he told me, "I'd be out there drinking and dancing."

He pulled a volume of Thomas Aquinas's *Summa Theologica* from a shelf and suggested I read Thomas's arguments for the immortality of the soul. I did, but not even Thomas could enlighten me.

Back at college I did not study the assigned readings; instead, I spent hours in the dark-paneled library reading Christopher Marlowe and whatever else I grabbed from library shelves.

At the end of spring term the college told me to take a year off. That was fine: I had had enough confinement. That summer I worked two months on a survey crew, then hitched west to Phoenix.

EIGHT
Boxcars West (summer 1963)

I was dwarfed by the boxcars towering over me, walking between lines of cars in the Phoenix freight yards, carrying a heavy pack. At eleven o'clock at night I was looking for the train that a switchman earlier that afternoon told me would leave at midnight, head south to Yuma, then northwest to L.A.

I clambered up and over a coupling between cars. I saw another switchman, dressed in jeans and Stetson hat, and asked where my freight was. He pointed to a tank car on a line being made up.

I trudged over to the train and found an open boxcar, threw my bag on the plank floor and hopped in. Lighting a match, I explored the dark recesses at both ends to see if there were other riders, or rats.

The train was still being made up. Every minute it cranked forward and then backed up with speed enough to hook onto a car behind, thousands of tons of metal slamming into metal.

Whenever it stopped pulling forward I was next to a freight

car full of winos, all howling to the night wind of the desert, drunk. They were on a car used for delivering autos, a mere skeleton, and had no protection from the wind. They wrapped themselves in cardboard. I was afraid of them, afraid they would wander over to my train and find me, or discover they were on the wrong freight and actually wanted mine. Our cars sat on adjacent tracks. I pictured them climbing into my car. There I would be, haunched in the back, trying to elude observation while they carried on. Finally one would say, "Let's find out what's in this car," light a match, see me and leer, "Hey, kid, what're you doing here?"

I would stammer, "Headin' for L.A., same as you, man." Then he would turn to his boys with lips curled over yellowed teeth, look back at me and say, "How much money you got on you?"

I did not unpack my sleeping bag. Instead, I sat on my pack near the open door, on the side opposite from them, ready to run.

Their train stood still, but mine moved back and forth with sudden stops and a SLAM! each time it added another car. This continued for an hour. Each time we pulled forward and stopped, I was opposite the bums. I kept looking at my watch, wondering how long before midnight and the freight pulled out. The air was frigid and there was nothing in the car to wrap around myself, nothing there except a few old orange crates and some two by fours, one of which I held expectantly.

Finally I heard voices. Brakemen approached, checking couplings. I could see their light as it arced back and forth with the swing of an arm. When they passed alongside my car one of them shone the light inside. He saw me and asked, "Goin' all the way?"

"You bet!" I said, and felt good.

Soon the train pulled out. Wanting to see all of Phoenix stretched out against the starlit night, I stood and leaned against the open door. We were pulling out slowly.

Somewhere near the outskirts of Phoenix we crossed a road with a red and white traffic guard lowered with cars behind it stopped. A couple sat in the first car. Exhilarated by the journey ahead, I waved to them and the woman waved back. I leaned out the boxcar, looked at the long line of freight cars behind, then went to the front of the car, out of the wind, and unpacked my sleeping bag. I stuffed all my clothes from my backpack inside it and slid in, and despite the hardness of the floor and the symphonic jazz crashing of the wheels and springs, slept well.

When I awoke the air was chill and wet with dawn. The east was pink. We were in southern Arizona. The land was sandy and covered with mesquite and cactus. I stayed comfortably curled in my bag until the air warmed.

By mid-morning we were entering a desert town. When I saw a cruel looking fortress atop a bluff I knew that was the Yuma Penitentiary, the prison of the Arizona Territory.

The train stopped at Yuma. I wondered for how long. I waited ten minutes before I jumped down, bringing my pack with me, slinging the straps through one arm and letting the pack bounce off a side of my back. I cut across the tracks to a water pipe with a faucet and drank. A hobo with a box of crackers sat on a crate beside the rails, munching. I asked him where he was going.

"South. Where you headed?"

"North to Bakersfield and into the Sierra Nevadas."

"Have some of these," he said and handed me the box of crackers.

Like many another 'bo his age was indeterminate. His face was a raw slab of meat, unshaven and weathered.

"What're you doing?" I asked him.

"Nothing, just travelin'. I had me a job coupla months ago as a cat operator. I made good money and when I got enough I left. Whenever I need money bad I do some dozer work. I got into this travelin' racket back east in Ohio when my wife left me. I said screw it. No point in bustin' myself over nothing."

I drank again from the faucet. As we sat talking he said, "Your train's leavin'." I looked up and saw it pulling out. I grabbed my pack and ran across the tracks until I got alongside my car. It was moving as fast as I could trot, and as I ran alongside the open door I wondered, "What if I sling my pack in and it slides all the way across the car and out the other door?" I took the straps in both hands, dumped it in and in one motion put my hands on the floor and swung in, off again across America, out into the blazing desert, the heat pouring into the open car.

That afternoon as I looked out of the car to the west I saw a huge sea. I said to myself, "A mirage! And what a mirage!" But it was not a mirage, as I later discovered, but the Salton Sea, the largest lake in the Southwest.

Soon afterwards, as we paralleled a highway, I saw signs reading, "Palm Springs Twenty Miles" and I thought of chic people, cocktails, and swimming pools and me in my shabby grimeclothes heading north for the wilderness.

We were in the Mojave Desert—bleak and desolate—but strung with towns every fifty miles or so. Hours later, mid-afternoon, we stopped at Indio, and as I sat on my pack smoking a cigarette and gazing across the land a Mexican kid came up and hoisted himself into the car. At first I distrusted him, but in time we began talking.

He said, "I was heading north weeth my family, my wife, her brother and his wife. Our car broke down. They said it was too long a trip to make. They wouldn't make it, so I'm going alone."

"Where are you going?"

"To the valley to work."

"What do you do?"

"Peek fruit."

"Where were you coming from?"

"Mejico."

He was not much older than I, and thin with dark brown skin and speech so convoluted and accented so strangely that at first I could not understand him. Later I became accustomed to his rhythms, his story breaks and lack of continuity. He offered me a cigarette, which I accepted. In fact we smoked his cigarettes all afternoon until he ran out, then started on my papers and tobacco. We sat at the edge of the car with no need to speak, just watching the land.

Around nightfall we were in the outskirts of L.A., moving slowly through freight yards with scores of tracks and redbrick warehouses with trucks parked alongside. The freight moved slowly past crowds of bums with huge parcels and belongings wrapped in canvas. One came running toward us, pounding his heavy thighs and feet onto the dirt and patches of grass, grunting and huffing loudly. He came alongside our car and the Mexican kid took the bundle from his outstretched hands. The bum threw himself upwards as he pushed with his hands off the floor, flung up a leg and landed in the car.

He was red-faced and lay down on the plank floor to recover. Later when he sat up, he pulled a pint of sherry from his jacket pocket and took long swigs. He offered us some. I told him no and the young Mexican shook his head. The bum did not say much, but sat near one end of the car, his back against the wall, talking to himself. Sometimes he looked at us and spoke, but I never understood him. Was he speaking to us? Or was he telling himself what he would do to us?

Around midnight we deadheaded in the L.A. yards, the first leg of my journey over.

The bum was heading north too. He knew his way around the yards. He warned us to stay in the boxcar and away from cops while he found a train. The young Mexican and I hung around the car until the bum returned furtively and told us to follow him. We crossed between cars over couplings, across rows of cars. Trains were everywhere. The yards were an amazing maze and tangle. At one point we came across a shack where the bum told us about a legendary hobo he called, "King of the Bums." At the shack we met another bo. Our bum asked him if he had seen Billy the Red, the legendary bum. He spoke of Billy the Red with awe, his words a faint gasp. This was hard to believe, because at other times our bum was a mad bull who would have thrown us off the rails if one of us had been alone in the car with him.

It was a freezing bitch of a night: cold teeth of steel and iron slivers cut through our clothes. The bum told us to scrounge for cardboard or we would freeze to death. He grabbed whatever was close by for himself. The young Mexican told me to wait in the car and he would get some. He disappeared into the night while I remained alert for cops, ready to dodge and run, while this mad bum slugged sherry. The Mexican returned with large sheets of cardboard.

Inside the car I slid into my sleeping bag and got on one edge of a cardboard sheet and rolled myself inside it, a cold security in a friendless jungle of cops, 'bo's and steel. But even so I went to sleep before the train pulled out. Hours later, it seemed, we were awakened by drunken bums wandering the yards. These were real gleam-eyed, knife carrying bums. They climbed into our car and sat between the doors, looking at us. Their leader, older than the others, was talking to our bum. I was too tired to realize our danger and was only barely conscious. Like me, the young Mexican said nothing. Our bum squared it with them and they left.

I remember us pulling out but then nothing until the next morning when we were in green hill country. We had left the city far behind us and were pulling over hills, winding slowly around them because of the drag of the open cars and the train's length. When we entered a tunnel I looked back and saw the train curling lazily around the side of the hill, and then, once out of the tunnel when I could look back, I saw from a high point the rest of the train on the other side of the hill crawling through.

By the time we were close to Bakersfield the bum was slugging from another bottle and getting nutty. Standing against a side of the car and facing the wall, he sometimes told me and sometimes the Mexican, "Come here, I've something to show you." His back was almost completely turned toward us. We stayed away from him.

When we arrived in Bakersfield, the young Mexican and I jumped off. I bid him farewell and headed for a road that crossed the tracks and entered Bakersfield. With no food for a day and a half, I was hungry. I went inside a drug store and had two hamburgers with a malt. Then I walked through downtown past white gas stations with pennants waving. At the outskirts I stuck my thumb out.

A man in a black Chevy stopped. We drove all the way to a big crossroads at the entrance to the national park. We were in the Sierra foothills, land covered with juniper and piñon and sparse clumps of grass. The driver was an old-timer who had lived in the woods with two friends mining silver, and when he heard that I planned camping for a month said, "If you can make it, great, but it's hard going." He then gave me a recipe for biscuits and let me off at a general store in a town that once was probably a lumber camp. The store window was filled with leather goods and fishing gear.

"Do you have a shovel?" he asked.

"No."

"Better get one. They won't let you in the park without one."

He had an air about him I respected. He, like the town, was in transition, somewhere between the old-time West of mining camps and the new efficient America.

NINE
The Sierra Nevadas (summer 1963)

I walked across the street and up the road to the ranger station—a log building—for a pass.

"How long you staying in?" a young ranger asked.

"A month. Got all my food right in here," I said, pointing to my pack on the floor. I was sure I would last a month.

"Wow!" he said.

He filled out my pass and gave me a grid map that would help me locate myself in the forest whenever I came upon a similar map printed on metal and nailed to a tree. Each map nailed to a tree had a mark to indicate its location.

From the ranger station I got a ride from a middle-aged couple. We passed over a wide, fast flowing river with fishermen dotting its banks. Once we crossed the bridge we entered the big woods. Tall pines with great girths succeeded the dwarf trees of the hills; a deep, soft gloom hung below their limbs. The couple was headed for Road's End, the last building on the road high in the mountains, a log cabin store, which once could be found on oil company maps of California.

At Road's End I got a ride from a lumberman and his son. The man named the trees that grew there, which ones were logged out and which were left. We drove with open windows; the smell of pines saturated the air. I was growing more anxious to get out and climb a mountain.

Further up the road, where they left me off, I strode into the forest and took the first trail I saw, not caring where it led. It took me upward through pinewoods mixed with birch and elm. Suddenly the trail widened, scraped flat. Heavy equipment sat nearby.

Other paths appeared, verging off. I picked one at random, following it until it disappeared into an under-growth of grass, leaves and twigs. My pack was heavy, I was sweating. The sun burned my neck, I pulled my collar up. Pushing aside branches and moving through mosquito swarms, I emerged above the timberline where large granite rocks thrust their heads through the earth. I was tired, the small of my back hurt.

I sat with my pack beside me and studied the tiny wild flowers that grew there. When I was rested and my back no longer hurt, I hiked to the peak. Pine slopes with rock outcroppings plunged to the valley hidden below. Far away loomed a great peak, which had to be Mt. Washington. I headed down the slope, fast, with a swinging stride.

Much later I found a stream where I unpacked my pots and dehydrated foods and built a fire. As the water heated my packet of shrimp Creole, I made myself a glass of powdered milk. The water boiled but, impatient and too hungry to wait and test the shrimp, I took them off the fire. They were hard and tasteless, I ate them anyway.

With a few hours of daylight left, I repacked and plunged on and up. Birds flitted through the pines; sunlight speckled the path. In the distance I heard rushing water, and by the sound knew it was no mere stream but a wild current. Hours later, drenched in sweat and with a back that ached, I saw it.

A cataract of water plunged down the mountain, fuming over huge rocks, sparkling in the sun between cool banks of pines. Near by, a stream off the cataract twisted into a pool. I stripped off my clothes and waded into the ice-cold water. After hesitating I sat, up to my chest. I dunked my head, jumped out and changed clothes.

Why did I not stay there, where I would have the solitude I wanted? Instead, I chose to head for Mt. Washington. I re-shouldered my pack and crossed the river, stepping slowly from rock to rock, while far down the mountain the river raged.

I climbed the steep bank opposite, holding onto roots and trunks. At the top of the ridge I headed west, following the river, hoping to find a map. I was now lost.

It was dusk when I dropped the pack, took out a pot and scrambled down the bank to the stream. I filled the small pot with water and built a fire in a clearing atop the bank. Once again I took the food off the fire before it was cooked.

As light disappeared I realized I had better make a shelter. Nearby lay a fallen pine, propped five feet off the ground by its branches. I found four long pine limbs with boughs and leaned them against the fallen pine and cut more boughs to make a soft flooring for my lean-to. I spread out my sleeping bag and stuffed it with dry clothes and slept.

I was jarred awake by a thundering that came crashing down the bank past my camp; something huge was thrashing madly across the ground. I grabbed my pathetic penknife I had laid beside me, open for just an occasion and yelled, hoping to scare it. It paid no attention, but continued its end of the world path down the slope. I waited in silence, afraid to lie down, listening for its return. Much later I lay down and slept, but the same noise awoke me. This time I was more frightened. The sound was coming right at me, even louder and more horrible. Again I bolted upright, grabbed my knife and yelled. This time the noise ceased abruptly. JESUS CHRIST! I thought. Sweat was pouring down me. I yelled again to get it the hell away and it worked. The beast bolted off into the brush.

Morning came chill but sweet. I realized how comfortable I felt lying in my sleeping bag on soft pine bedding. From the end of my lean-to I could see the top of the hill where I had cooked the night before. Blue smoke drifted skyward. I looked at it, probably still smiling, when I realized with a shock that the smoke came from last night's fire. I scrambled out of my sleeping bag, put on shoes and ran to the top. I had cooked my meal on a bank of peat moss. This nice cleared spot had once been a log that had rotted into such fine particles that at dusk it looked like earth.

I ran for my pot, slid down the bank to the pounding stream, filled it and struggled back up and dumped water on the smoldering peat. I scrambled down for more water and repeated the process again and again. I dug a circle around the peat to keep it from spreading. I realized that the fire could smolder under it. I dug deeper and mixed in sand. The peat was very warm. CHRIST! More water! More sand! I worked for an hour, digging in all directions away from it, churning up the peat, digging ever deeper and continuing to pour water on it, then more sand. Finally, when I could not feel any heat, I packed and left.

I followed the bank downhill to the path I had taken yesterday and I felt easy again. The air warmed and I began sweating; I had visions of outdoor suburban house parties with long tables of food. I saw cold watermelons sliced in quarters and cantaloupes cut into slivers. I saw piles of cherries and grapes.

Whenever I came to a stream I drank big gulps until my stomach swelled painfully. At one stream I saw cement block fireplaces. Further on, I saw horse tracks and a sign for a boys' camp. Soon I came upon bags of food suspended from tree limbs. Without intending it, I was heading back to people.

The path twisted and climbed. My legs burned. As I neared the top of one turn I heard motorbikes approach. Motorbikes in the forest! Still, I wished I had one. I had ruined my trip with ceaseless hiking. If I had made camp and stayed put, I could have lasted many more days. Instead, I wanted to climb Mt. Washington.

Casual strollers in shorts appeared. I came to the campground where the lumberman left me off the day before. It was filled with trailers. Families from L.A., Frisco and elsewhere thronged there, each of them yelling. Mothers were shouting at kids who were playing tag and ball, ordering them to come eat. Since they brought the city with them, I wondered why they came. It did not occur to me that my own failure was theirs: that I, too, had brought the impatience of urban life with me.

I picked a spot and cooked my dinner near a large hollow log. After I ate, I cut pine boughs and put them inside the log, then my sleeping bag, feet side facing out. Later, when I crawled in, I had my best sleep in days.

The next morning I awoke to the smell of wood smoke and

food. I cooked a final meal of pancakes and cocoa, then packed everything, except the food. I approached an older couple and asked if they could use it. They took it and thanked me.

I had failed at something I wanted very much to do, and did not realize why.

TEN

On the Road (Summer 1963)

Two rides took me into Bakersfield. I was broke. I hadn't a penny and I was hungry. I stopped the first man I met and said, "Could you stake me to a meal?" It was a line inspired by the movie, *Treasure of the Sierra Madre*, in which Bogart asks a man, "Say, pal, could you stake a fellow American to a meal?" The man looked Mexican. He looked at me and said no. I walked on and he disappeared into a store. Seconds later he ran up behind me and said, "Here, get yourself something to eat," and handed me fifty cents. I thanked him and walked on. The fifty cents would buy me a sandwich and a Coke, but I wanted more food. I saw a farmer in overalls walking towards me and gave him the same line. He gave me a quarter. With my money I went into a luncheonette and had a tuna fish sandwich, a Coke and a candy bar, with change still left.

I walked to the tracks where I stood around the yard office, waiting to ask a railroader for a connection back to L.A. I spotted an engine slowly making its way towards me, with an engineer and a fireman my age aboard.

I bolted over, walking alongside the engine and asked the kid, "When's the next train to L.A.?"

"Eleven tonight. Five tracks over."

"Thanks."

"You better get yourself some water for the trip. It's going to be a long one."

"Okay, thanks."

I found two Coke bottles near a water pipe at the yard office, filled them and made my way over to the train. There were no empty boxcars. The train from Phoenix had empty cars because it was deadheading. This one had cargo. I found an empty gondola and climbed up the rungs.

Horns blared, trains clanged back and forth and cars ran overhead on the nearby highway. I was thinking of what everyone across America was doing. And there I was, squatting in a gondola, happy, dreaming, sure that the future was going to be good, musing till the sun went down and the kid fireman came running across the tracks with two hamburgers and a malted milk, saying, "I brought you these things to eat. I felt kinda bad. Here I am making $120 a week for doing nothing. I don't need all this money. You take some."

That was one of the big surprises and kindnesses of the trip.

"I'll be back with more," he said and sped off into the darkness. And he did return, with three chocolate bars and another large malted. We talked some more. He was a college student who lived in the suburbs around Bakersfield. At the end of our conversation I asked for his address, said I would write and pay him back.

The next day broke over my poor skull with a crash. The heat of the Mojave desert melted whatever brains I had. Sitting on my pack in the gondola under the scorching sun, I devised a means to get rich quick in Phoenix. I reasoned that since in ten minutes in Bakersfield I had raised seventy-five cents, I could make possibly as much as thirty-six dollars just for a morning's work in Phoenix. I planned my daily schedule for Phoenix. I would get up at 8:00, have breakfast, and by 9:00—wearing my road clothes—would start panhandling. I would panhandle until 1:00. After a few days of panhandling I would have enough money to buy a seersucker suit. (By this time I would also be living in a hotel.) After 1:00 I would change from my rags into my suit and head to the library for an afternoon of study and reading and, of course, polite conversation with my literary friends. Afterwards I would cut out for dinner in a posh southwestern restaurant where I would dine in the soft glow of red lamplight. This was what I was actually thinking as I rattled in my gondola.

For four hours I rode through the Mojave in the relentless sun without a hat, but finally draped a shirt over my head. The Mojave camp with bo's scattered about, lying on shirts, chests naked to the sun, a crowd of them sitting near a faucet under which one bare-chested bum sat, letting the water run over his head and down his torso while the others waited. Another bo tried to butt in but the bum under the faucet shoved him viciously away.

I watched clusters of hoodlum bo's with long blonde hair and muscled chests walk with large sheets of cardboard folded under their arms, two or three of them carrying sheets for warmth that night.

I wandered off the tracks to the yards and the town where crates of grapes were being shipped off, vast stacks of green grapes lying in piles on tables before being crated. I wanted to take just one grape but did not dare. I just looked.

I walked back to my train and climbed up the rungs of my gondola. The train pulled out, exposing me to four more hours in the blasting sun. Finally it slowed near a gas station, giving precedence to an approaching train. It waited so long that I hopped off the car and carried my pack a quarter mile across the desert to the gas station. I went into the men's room and put my head under the sink and let it run. I took off my shirt and splashed myself with water to remove the grit and sweat. There were no paper towels. I went outside and asked the attendant for some.

"We don't give towels with our showers," he told me.

The gas station was crowded with drivers. A reporter for *Life* magazine stood inside a phone booth calling his boss about an interview. There was a couple in a sports car and a trucker heading south. I asked him if he would give me a lift.

"As far as Kingman, Arizona," he told me. "There's an I.C.C. checkpoint there and I can't give you a ride beyond. I'd lose my job."

I climbed in the cab and we roared off. Both windows were rolled down to cut the heat, but it was no use, the air blasted in like a furnace. It was the most miserable ride I had ever had in my life, but it was faster than the train. The trucker let me off at Kingman at sundown. I walked down the highway to the railroad tracks.

The sun had streaked the clouds purple. Kingman looked dismal. I had felt this before in other whistle-stop towns, where was sand, nothing but sand could I see except for the mountains to the east. A sign on the nearby highway pointed to Mitchell's Cavern. I had read about Mitchell's Cavern—a cave with a perpendicular drop to which no bottom had been found.

At one point the train stopped at a town with a regular hobo camp with bo's scattered about, lying on shirts, chests naked to the sun, a crowd of them sitting near a faucet under which one barechested bum sat, letting the water run over his head and down his torso while the others waited. Another bo tried to butt in but the bum under the faucet shoved him viciously away.

I watched clusters of hoodlum bo's with long blonde hair and muscled chests walk with large sheets of cardboard folded under their arms, two or three of them carrying sheets for warmth that night.

I wandered off the tracks to the yards and the town where crates of grapes were being shipped off, vast stacks of green grapes lying in piles on tables before being crated. I wanted to take just one grape but did not dare. I just looked.

I walked back to my train and climbed up the rungs of my gondola. The train pulled out, exposing me to four more hours in the blasting sun. Finally it slowed near a gas station, giving precedence to an approaching train. It waited so long that I hopped off the car and carried my pack a quarter mile across the desert to the gas station. I went into the men's room and put my head under the sink and let it run. I took off my shirt and splashed myself with water to remove the grit and sweat. There were no paper towels. I went outside and asked the attendant for some.

"We don't give towels with our showers," he told me.

The gas station was crowded with drivers. A reporter for *Life* magazine stood inside a phone booth calling his boss about an interview. There was a couple in a sports car and a trucker heading south. I asked him if he would give me a lift.

"As far as Kingman, Arizona," he told me. "There's an I.C.C. checkpoint there and I can't give you a ride beyond. I'd lose my job."

I climbed in the cab and we roared off. Both windows were rolled down to cut the heat, but it was no use, the air blasted in like a furnace. It was the most miserable ride I had ever had in my life, but it was faster than the train. The trucker let me off at Kingman at sundown. I walked down the highway to the railroad tracks. The sun had streaked the clouds purple. Kingman looked dismal. I had felt this before in other whistle-stop towns, where it looks like the end of the line for everybody. You wonder why anyone came to live there and why they stay.

At Kingman I got a ride from a short, thin man with blonde hair and no chin. He told me his life story.

"I went into the war at nineteen, a bomber pilot on a B-26. It completely wrecked me. When I came back I got married. I never should have. The marriage didn't last five years.

"I've never gotten over the war. I tried selling, and I kept at it for a while, but I broke down and that's when my wife and I got a divorce."

He went on, telling me he was heading for Tucson and was passing by Phoenix. He would let me off there. He looked at me. He said, "You look like you need a rest, son. Why don't you come to Tucson with me? I'm going to be there a few days. I'll get you a place to stay. If you want, you can come back to Los Angeles with me. You don't have to stay at my place. I'll get you your own. I won't even disturb you."

I told him no, that I had other plans.

When we got close to Phoenix he stopped for gas and bought us Cokes. I noticed he was wearing tight white Levies and sneakers. I wanted to believe the best of him but when I saw that outfit I knew he was wrong.

When we arrived in Phoenix he told me, "I hope you'll change your mind and go on to Tucson. You got nowhere to stay here. You need a good bath of hot water and a rubdown." He emphasized the last word.

"No," I said, "I don't think so."

When he left me off on the outskirts of town he told me the name of the motel he was staying at, in case I changed my mind. He said I should call him collect. He left me off in the skid-row section of Phoenix, where I wandered until I found a park and lay down under trees for the night. The streetlights illuminated the outskirts of the park, but except for the possibility of a wandering patrolman I felt I would be left undisturbed. The air was chill, but I did not dare unpack my sleeping bag. If cops approached I wanted to run. With cars swishing past and midnight voices lingering in the air, I slept but fitfully.

When morning came I was already sitting on one of the benches, waiting to spot a prospect. I saw some walk into a luncheonette across the square and ambled over and asked the next man I saw if he would stake me to a meal. He looked at me, said no and walked away. Then, as happened in Bakersfield, he came back. He took me in the dinner, ordered a meal for me, paid the cashier and left without saying a word. The waitress was kind and I was fed a stack of pancakes with plenty of butter, bacon and eggs, milk and coffee. When I left all I could do was blush at the waitress and say good-bye to the cashier. What politeness to a kid who smelled of coal, pinesap, dust and sweat!

I was drawn back to the park, partly out of curiosity to meet the denizens, and partly to find my way around. At the park I sat on a bench next to a chubby man with hornrim glasses and very thick lenses. His name was John. He, too, wanted to tell me his story.

"I came into this town three days ago with my wife," he said. "We parked the car, got ourselves a hotel room. Then she excused herself, told me she had some things to do. I haven't seen her since. When she didn't come back to the hotel that afternoon I went searching for her. The old lady's an alcoholic. I gave her description to bartenders and one of them said they'd seen her in there all one day—boozing. Then she took off. Goddamn if she didn't take the car and all of our clothes and sell 'em for money to buy more booze with. She'd been off the stuff for a while, but this did it. Now she's back on, with all my money."

He was wearing a disheveled suit. His shirt was wrinkled and his face was unshaven. He leaned back against the bench with his arms sprawled on it. Then he leaned forward, putting his elbows on his knees and spat.

"Ah, shit," he said. "The no-good fool."

He looked up at me.

"She's done this before. Last time was in Kansas City, but I caught her after the third day, just went from bar to bar and back again until I found her."

He took out rolling papers and a sack of Bull Durham. He looked up at me as I smoked a Camel.

"You gotta watch yourself, kid. Don't let any of these guys see you've got yourself ready-rolled smokes. They'll all start borrowin' from you until you ain't got nothin' left."

He rolled his cigarette and looked on either side of himself, as if to see if there were other bums around. Soon John was asking me for cigarettes.

"You come with me this afternoon for a meal at St. Vincent de Paul's."

"What's that?"

"It's the mission here. They give out free meals at noon everyday. Plenty of people there."

We strolled over to St. Vincent's at noon. Standing on the sidewalk in front of the whitewashed, two-story structure was the most colorful crew I had ever seen—a mob of Indians, Mexicans, and Anglos—bums and hobos, elderly folks on the down and out, young women with kids. Long haired Mexicans and Indians in purple shirts and jeans and wild scarves wound around brown, creased necks stood next to old bo's in red-checked shirts with pot bellies sagging over frayed belts, and wearing broken, scuffed shoes. Amid all these stood young, gaunt-faced girls in loose-fitting gowns with children clutching their mother's dresses with little fists.

John walked over to a small knot of men. One, I noticed, must have been Red, an old-timer John had earlier said would help me out. Red was about five-eight with red hair, a flabby paunch and an alcoholic face with sagging cheeks and bloodshot eyes. After mingling with some more of the boys, John came over and told me to step over with him to meet Red.

Red moved directly in front of me.

"Where you from, boy?" he asked.

"Connecticut."

"How old are you?"

"Nineteen."

"Nineteen, boy!"

Red's hangdog eyes were now glaring at me, flashing with anger.

"Go home! Go home! Get out of this racket. It STINKS! You're too young and stupid to know it."

"I like it."

Red became angrier. "I did it and I never went back!" he shouted. "Take it from me, it stinks!" Then, calmly, he asked, "Do you have parents?"

"Yes."

A second later his mood changed again and he was once more yelling. I was somewhat afraid of him, not because I thought he would take a swing at me, but for his strange unpredictability.

"I can stand here looking at you and know that you're stupid and don't know what you're doing. Go back home now. Don't waste your life! Go back before it's too late and you end up like THESE BUMS!"

Red flung his arms about, indicating all the men and women in the crowd—the old men with hands in pockets, not caring; the laughing, white-teethed Mexicans, laughing out of strength; the bewildered and frightened women who wondered what would happen to themselves and their kids.

Red was so mad and wound up he was spewing spittle in my face. The veins in his neck were popping. When I backed off he stopped talking and turned round into the crowd.

John returned. The mission doors opened and we lined up.

By the time John and I got inside, the line extended from the front doors down the 100-foot sidewall to the servers. The walls were white and the room was filled with rows of big tables and benches. Already men were lumbering to the benches with tin plates of food. When I finally reached the front of the line I got myself a tin plate and plastic cup. I was given a powdered drink, pinto beans, a tortilla, and a boiled potato with skin. I sat with John, Red, and one of their friends. The food was dry, about the worst I ever ate.

Far from being depressed by this scene, I was straining to see and hear everything.

After lunch John and I cut back to the park where he instructed me further in the means of getting on as a bum.

"I've been staying at the Salvation Army. They give you two nights a week. I've already used up one."

"Is it free?" I asked.

"Of course," he said. "You've got to sign in by four o'clock."

We spent several hours talking before I went to the Salvation Army and registered for the night. I got there before it opened. A young man in his twenties with an Air Force bag was standing outside. We sat on our bags and smoked while we waited. When the doors opened I went in, signed my name to the register and stowed my pack. They said I had to be back by five o'clock and no later.

I walked off downtown to panhandle and look around. In the Mexican section I approached a Negro who handed me ten cents, but another Negro and a Mexican just shook their heads. I cursed. I was beginning to see my hopes dashed. I walked into a better section of town where the buildings were taller, the traffic heavier, where middle-class suburban housewives shopped. Still no luck. Most of the passersby would not even look at me.

I walked to the library where I read until four-thirty and then walked several miles back to the Salvation Army. John was there. So were some of the others I had seen at St. Vincent's. The Salvation Army captain or major told us that we had to take showers, and others led us into an anteroom where we stripped and were handed towels and soap. After the shower I changed back into my road clothes. We were led into the dining room where we stood on line for hotdogs and chili, which were almost as bad as the pinto beans and boiled potato at St. Vincent's. I groused about it to John, but remembered that a few days before I had bitched to a withered bum about the cigarette he had rolled me.

Before we ate the major led us in prayer. Then we were handed hymnals and he and some of the Salvation Army women led us in songs which everyone sung halfheartedly, except for the major and the women who were trying to pitch some religion into our souls.

After dinner we sat on our bunks batting the breeze and smoking until lights-out at nine o'clock. The next morning after they fed us breakfast, John told me how bums made enough to get a flop for a week.

"They go down to the blood bank and sell a pint for four bucks. That's where I'm going this morning. They only let you sell a pint once every week and I haven't sold any yet, so I can do it. These other guys go down every morning and try it. Most of them get kicked out."

"Yeah," Red said, "there's a real bitch down there who checks 'em over real careful, won't let most of them sell till the time's up. Come on down with us. You ain't old enough to sell blood, but maybe they won't ask you for your I.D."

The three of us trudged across the park and down a block to a small building where other bums sat around on couches, waiting. Several were having long arguments with the lady—the "bitch"— swearing they had not been in that week. She kicked them all out. I was sitting in a chair, sweating; bureaucrats intimidated me. I walked up and said I wanted to sell a pint.

"How old are you?" she asked.

"Twenty-one."

"Let's see your identification."

"I don't have it. I lost my wallet."

"Sorry, but in that case we can't accept you."

I told John I would wait outside.

Both he and Red sold their blood and when they came out they were happy and assumed a superior air. They made jokes and talked to each other and ignored me. I was tired of their company anyway, and wanted something new. I bid them farewell. Stunned that I was unable to raise any money panhandling, I decided to head home. I trudged across Phoenix, which in those days was still a small cowtown, to a highway heading northeast. I was on my way back across America.

My first ride was with an old man that swung me across stretches of desert clear to Globe, Arizona. There he left me off at a roadside park where I was most likely to get a ride. Lots of cars were parked there with their owners at benches eating lunch.

One old couple told me they would not give rides to hitch-hikers but the old man gave me several baloney and onion sandwiches and some pastries. I put them in my jacket pockets and wandered over to a younger couple. The woman was wearing a light terry cloth blouse that started just below her breasts and outlined her wonderful shape. Her husband was a wiry guy browned from the sun. They asked me to sit down.

"Where are you going?" they asked.

"All the way to Connecticut."

"Sure, we'll give you a ride."

When we took off they told me they would not have given me a ride except that I was carrying a pack.

"Bumming is a joyous thing," the man said. "It's lark and a man should carry a pack. I don't trust those who carry suitcases. It sort of means they're not doing it for fun. They're trying to get someplace. Do you see what I mean?"

"Yep, I agree."

"We're from Australia."

"You are? You don't have the accent."

"That's overplayed. It's all a bunch of nonsense. We're been traveling around the world, working when we need money. We just came from Canada. I worked as a carpenter there while my wife waitressed. We're been all through Europe, now we're going to Mexico to see the bullfights."

"But this is the wrong time of the year," I told him. "The bullfights are only in winter. You've missed them."

This was not true, but was what I had heard. I hoped that by telling them they might decide to swing east and carry me a thousand miles closer to my destination.

"Oh, really? We didn't know that. Huh. Maybe we'll go to Tucson and figure things from there."

And that's precisely what they did. They left me off in a town north of Tucson, a tough little camp where I went into a diner. I still had some change left from Bakersfield, enough to buy a sandwich. There I saw a man eating lunch who I thought might be traveling east. When he left I gobbled my meal, lurched after him, and asked for a lift.

"Yes. Get in."

When I saw his car, I realized he was a sheriff. He was laconic and taciturn; I leaned back and relaxed. When we got to a river that passed under the highway, he cut across the road and parked.

"Going to check the river."

As I followed him down the bank to the river, I became apprehensive. Why were we going to the riverbank? Why did he park his car where it was screened by cottonwoods and could not be seen from the road? But he only knelt and looked in the water.

"I'm thinking of bringing the kids down here fishing and camping. The fishing looks good."

I sighed with relief.

We got back in the car and drove a hundred miles down the road. I picked up my next ride from a trucker who drove until late that night. He pulled over near a gas station.

"I'm going to sleep," he said. "I like to sleep on the hood where I can get air."

I knew how cold the night air was.

"Say," I said, "I'll sleep there. You don't have to."

"I like it. I sleep better out there than inside. You take the cab."

He got his blankets and stretched them out on the cab's wide hood while I put my head back on the seat and slept, but not for long. Soon I was outside pitching pebbles. We were parked on the outskirts of a town. I was getting tired of waiting, but I did not think I would have much luck getting another ride that late. I went back inside the cab and slept until dawn, when the trucker climbed back in and we roared off across the rest of Arizona on Route 66 into New Mexico.

I stayed on 66 into the flat grasslands of the Oklahoma Panhandle and Kansas, heading for Missouri. I was bone tired after so many days on the road. I decided to head for my uncle Bob's home in St. Louis for a rest. The next night, inside a café on 66 in Missouri where my last ride left me off, I got a lift from a friendly but dumb kid who drove me several hundred miles. Whenever he stopped, I napped. He left me at a café where I hooked up with a trucker headed for St. Louis. I was utterly beat. After days of sitting, my legs were stiff with cramp and my back was sore. We stopped for coffee and lurched off into the dawn, past farmhouses shrouded in mist.

He dropped me off a few miles outside St. Louis, where I got a ride from a dynamiter, who left me in a Negro neighborhood about eight in the morning. I shouldered my pack and walked into a Saturday morning bar where a few hardtime drinkers were getting set for another day. I called my uncle, whom I had not seen since the years when he and his wife, Mary, lived in New Jersey. Mary answered the phone. I told her where I was and she came and got me.

Bob looked very much like my father in build and face, but heavier. He was a big man with a thick shock of hair and a bellowing laugh and broad smile that seemed the epitome of heartland America.

That afternoon Mary washed my clothes while I slept. Dinner that evening was a big meal of corn, steak and salad, a meal that tasted so good after the last few weeks' food that I ate until my stomach hurt. The next day, Sunday, I cut their lawn. On Monday morning Bob loaned me five dollars and drove me to Route 66.

I stayed on 66 to Chicago, where I crossed into Indiana and took the toll roads. A succession of rides took me through the Indiana and Ohio prairies, flat and dull, and into rolling Pennsylvania with its endless eastern woods. On the New Jersey Turnpike I picked up a ride from a Negro driving a huge, lumbering U.S. postal truck. He could have lost his job giving me a ride, but he drove me to Union City, talking incessantly. We passed miles of oil refineries that lay outside New Jersey's massive sprawling cities, covered with thick noxious fumes.

"You want a job driving one of these rigs?" he asked me.

"I don't know anything about them," I shouted back. "Not the first thing."

"You can learn. You can get yourself a job driving the run from Hoboken to Philly every day."

I thought about it.

When we got to the loading ramps in the huge terminal he backed it up. Other Negroes there started loading the trailer. He gave me his address in Brooklyn and told me to call him. I thanked him and walked off, wondering how I was now going to get to Manhattan with all my money spent and nothing to pay for a bus ride. I walked over to the entrance to the Holland Tunnel and stuck out my thumb. One ride shot me clear into downtown Manhattan, a dreary place after the space of the West.

I wandered through west side deserted streets between high piled buildings, walking towards Madison Avenue to my father's office. Conspicuous amid the businessmen in expensive suits, I felt slightly ashamed, especially as the company receptionist did not know what to make of me. I said I wanted Mr. Wolf and he came out, smiling and gave me money for the train home, but later told me never to do that again, that it gave clients a bad impression of the office.

So I was home from my travels and what I needed was a job. I returned to the survey company I had worked for earlier, and stayed until late January, when I decided to return to a village in New Mexico I had visited for thirty minutes that summer—Duran.

ELEVEN
Duran, New Mexico (1963)

A forty-five revolver hangs by a nail on the wall through its trigger guard. Beneath it a small sign reads, "Yessir, this ain't the gun that killed Billy the Kid."

I am standing by the cash register in a general store in Duran. I have gotten a ride from Indiana all the way to Duran from a young journalist and wise guy who carries a pistol in his glove compartment. He's on his way to Las Vegas to gamble. I'm on my way to San Francisco. We have made it here driving straight through, heading west from Indiana until somewhere on Route 66 near Tucumcari he decides that he wants to see Mexico and thinks we might drive there in an hour or two. He does not have a map.

At Vaughn we swing south. I know it is a longer detour to

Mexico than he thinks, but going or not is up to him. I am game either way. Thirty miles south of Vaughn we stop at Duran, at the general store on the edge of the highway to ask how long it will take us to drive to Mexico. Duran is a village of stuccoed houses with tin roofs and dirt yards.

This general store has shelves piled with tins of fruit and vegetables, shelves of hardware, racks of clothes (including a table filled with U.S. Calvary flat brimmed hats) and tack for horsemen. Mexicans hang around the store, drinking pop and smoking cigarettes. They pay no attention to us.

With the small store, the tin-roofed houses, and stone post office, Duran looks like it might be plunked down in the 1880s when the Kid was rustling cattle across the region from here to Lincoln County and into Texas. Now, seeing the sign above the counter I say to myself, "I'm coming back to stay awhile."

Flash forward seven months. I'm headed for Duran. I have ridden the Santa Fe Railroad from Chicago to Vaughn and at Vaughn stick out my thumb. I have worked much of the previous seven months running a transit for a survey company while living with my parents and saving money. In early February I pack my rucksack and take the train to New York's Grand Central Station and board the Twentieth Century Limited to Chicago.

For some reason, known only to a nineteen-year-old mind nurtured in suburban Connecticut, I am wearing a three-piece corduroy suit. So I am standing outside Vaughn in this suit and a rucksack on my back, thumb stuck out. A battered pickup stops. A very dark Indian-looking Mexican-American is driving, accompanied by an old man. I squeeze into the cab. They speak heavily accented English and live in Duran.

Thirty minutes later they drop me off at the general store owned by Ahmed Hamra, a small Lebanese man with skin the color of sand.

"I'm looking to rent a room," I tell Ahmed.

There is a small cluster of men in the store looking at this newcomer. Ahmed speaks to them in Spanish. They talk among themselves and Ahmed tells me to see someone named Memo—he has an extra room.

I walk down a dirt street to a house with a fenced-in yard and open the wire gate. Memo is big, fat. His wife and daughter are sized to match him. Memo shows me a room with a bed, chair and desk and names a price. It is more than I want to spend, but since I am wearing a corduroy suit, I am obviously rich. I tell Memo no and walk back to Ahmed's.

"It's too expensive," I tell Ahmed. "Is there anything else?"

"I have two cabins," Ahmed says. "Come on."

Right beside his general store are two small cabins. He unlocks the padlock on one. This is a one-room shack with a cast-iron cookstove, a bed and mattress, a small, unpainted desk, a cracked chair and a light bulb on the ceiling with a dangling pull string. There is nothing to the walls except the exterior wood.

"How much?"

"Ten dollars a month," Ahmed tells me.

"There's no water," I say.

"I'll loan you a bucket."

"All right."

I think this is a great deal. I have no idea how cold the nights will be. I have never heated with a wood stove and do not understand that you cannot heat a room with a cook stove, let alone heat a room in winter with wind seeping through the walls and a fire that will not last more than a half hour.

I do not have an axe to cut wood. I do not have a frying pan or pot, plates or utensils. I go back to Ahmed's, pay him ten dollars and buy some cans of food, a frying pan and pot. Then I go back to the cabin and make some notes in a journal. That night, the first of many, I sleep fully clothed in my sleeping bag with all my other clothes stuffed inside. When the fire goes out I don't crawl out of the bag to rekindle another. It is just too cold. In the morning the water in my bucket is frozen.

During the days I try to write, but I can't. It's too cold to concentrate. I do no more than make a few journal entries and notes for a play. Most of the time I sit and shiver at my desk, watching my breath make plumes of steam.

When the five or six local boys are not in school, they hang out at my shack. It gets even harder to concentrate. They ask me questions, some, but not many. Where am I from? Why am I there? They have never met anyone like me, nor I anyone like them. At their second or third visit, after a snow, they see how cold I am and that I do not know how to make a proper fire in the stove. I simply fill the space under the lids with kindling and paper and a few small branches and wait five minutes until they burn out. They leave and come back, dragging small juniper and piñon limbs, making a big stack of wood in the yard. The youngest boy, Billy Lucero, does most of the chopping. They have brought newspaper and show me how to make a proper fire in the stove. Still, it does not throw enough heat to warm the room.

I learn to lock my door when I discover that the kids have visited the cabin and read the journal in which I described the men who gave me a ride to Duran as "Mexican." "We're Mexican-Americans," they tell me.

Since it's too cold to stay in the cabin and write, I spend my days at the general store, smoking Lucky Strikes, listening to the old men, and watching their gestures. Out of politeness they will sometimes speak English, but mostly it's Spanglish, a mixture of the two languages. One of the men I get to know is the small, dark Indian-looking man who drove me to Duran. His name is Manuel Chavez.

Manuel's father was part Apache, a drunk who periodically arrived unexpectedly in Duran. When Manuel was young his father often beat him and even now threatened Manuel whenever he came to Duran. Manuel, when I first met him, was in his early forties and still lived in fear of his father.

I began to know Manuel during the days when he and I and the older men of Duran sat in Ahmed's store drinking coffee and smoking. The old men teased Manuel. They teased him, I think, because they could get a rise out of him and perhaps because he looked different from most of them. His was dark and he wore glasses with thick lenses and his upper teeth protruded.

Manuel also limped. He had been in a highway crash, in a pickup driven by a friend. The pickup's cab had been nearly destroyed and Manuel's right leg had been shattered and was now held together with pins.

There was nothing else for the old men to do except sit around Ahmed's store. Like the town itself, the people of Duran just hung on.

It had not always been so. The Southern Pacific Railroad had tracks running south from Vaughn past Duran, paralleling Highway 54. Years ago, Duran had a Southern Pacific roundhouse for engine and car repair. The roundhouse had been torn down long ago and all that now lay beyond the Southern Pacific tracks across from Duran were an abandoned two-story mercantile store and a gravel road that led from Duran fifteen miles to Estancia, another wisp of a town. Once the roundhouse was torn down, Duran began dying.

By 1963 the three operating businesses in town were the post office—a small stone building—Ahmed's general store, and George Hamra's bar, which was open only on Saturday nights, and then only occasionally.

The Hamras were Lebanese and had arrived in America in the early twentieth century, before the First World War. They raised sheep and were said to raise the finest Arabian horses in America.

Ahmed was uncle to George and Elias Hamra. Elias was in charge of the Hamra ranch. I saw George only on Saturday nights at his bar and Elias but seldom, and at a distance, in his pickup.

Most of the men and boys from town came to George's on the Saturday nights he was open. The women did not come to George's.

For Manuel and I, George's bar was where we had the most fun of the week. Manuel was not supposed to drink but he did, but only once a week, whenever George's bar was open. He was not supposed to drink because he had a bad stomach and always suffered the next day. One early morning, after a night at George's, Manuel was outside the trailer, splitting wood. He felt miserable. He put down the axe, and retched. A woman saw this and told him, "Why don't you drink some more, so you can throw up again?" Neither of us knew how to drink cautiously, slowly. We would each buy a quart of beer, and when we finished that, buy another. We drank them steadily.

George's bar had a pool table. Manuel and I were miserable players but we loved the game. We were such miserable pool players, especially when we had drunk too many quarts, that everyone in the bar watched us, shouted comments and laughed. I think watching us play pool was their big kick of the week. Even kind-hearted, fat Memo roared with good-natured laughter at our antics at the pool table.

All the men and boys from the Lucero family came. The Lucero kids, Arturo and Billy, and their friends, including the twenty-something year old Benny who was crippled in one arm, hung together in the evenings and came to the bar on Saturday nights.

Luis Lucero, in his late twenties or early thirties, was the eldest of the Lucero boys. Unlike his brothers, Luis was quiet and serious. He was married and lived with his wife on the edge of the village. He came to the bar.

Armando, the town postmaster, a jolly man with a paunch (who the boys called Tubby) would come. His brother. Enrique, a somber-looking man, also showed up. So did Memo—big, kind-hearted, fat Memo.

If Manuel hit one of my balls into a pocket, someone would shout, "Hey! Manuel! Wrong color, primo! Get yourself a new pair of glasses!" and everyone would roar and cackle. Manuel did have thick glasses.

"That man is blind!" someone would say.

Depending on his mood, Manuel might turn and smile or else might say, "Eef you think you can do any better, les see you!" which made the men cackle even louder.

With two beers Manuel became light-hearted. After three he began walking unsteadily. He would get soft and cry. Anything might set him off. Almost as much fun for the men as watching us play pool was to say something that would set Manuel to crying.

I began to spend time with Manuel at his tiny trailer, watching and later helping him cook simple meals of beef, potatoes and tortillas with powdered red chili. Manuel had stomach ulcers and could not eat hot peppers. If he ate a hot pepper he would hold his stomach and have to lie down. It was the same when he drank beer.

After Manuel and I cooked dinner in his trailer, we waited for the town kids and Benny to show up. Two of the Lucero brothers, Arturo and Billy, would come. Altogether there were about five kids, and nice kids they were. Arturo though, already an adolescent and five or six older than Billy, was already becoming closed and angry. Many years later he would tell me how the family picked watermelons in summers moving about Texas and how they were treated by the whites and his anger would rise. From the time he was Jimmy's age he had known the humiliation of being told to sit in a segregated section of a Texas movie theater. But my knowing this was not to be for many years, and for the time being in the evenings after dinner we all sat around Manuel's small woodstove in his tiny trailer, not knowing much about each other.

Nearly a week after I arrived in February, the kids were talking excitedly about a new British singing group that had appeared on the Ed Sullivan show. I had not heard of the group, but Arturo and Billy and the others had, and had heard one of the group's songs. "I Want to Hold Your Hand" that had been getting a lot of airplay. But since I did not own a radio, I knew nothing about the song or the group. I learned about The Beatles from the kids, after they had seen them on "The Ed Sullivan Show" and talked excitedly about them the next day.

I was puzzled that the kids would be interested, even excited, by The Beatles—they and their music seemed so alien to the life of this tiny village. What had the culture of Duran in common with that of England, or New York, or any place outside its own landscape? Here the boys were, thirty miles from the nearest town, in a sparsely populated state, and the music and appearance of these young foreign musicians aroused their interest. In all the time I spent in Duran, this was the most excited I ever saw them. Looking back on it even now, it still seems strange, but then the spread of white culture across the world continues to puzzle me.

Although most everyone in Duran loved to gossip about everyone else in town, no one, not even the boys, asked me much of anything about where I had grown up. They had some questions, but they were not curious about what the town I lived in was like or what my people were like. But then I knew little about them and never asked them much either. The only man I knew anything about was Manuel.

When I first went to live in Duran, perhaps sixty-five people, mostly old, lived there. The Lucero kids, including Arturo and Billy, were the youngest. The only girl in town was Louisa, who was sweet and fat. There was one young woman, Lucero's wife. All the others were either middle-aged or old.

Armando, the postmaster, was middle-aged. His brother, Enrique, was somewhat older and was a janitor in Vaughn. Memo drove the school bus back and forth from Vaughn. He was in his early fifties. Manuel had been the janitor at the Duran school but now that was closed. The rest of the few men in Duran were too old to work, or like Benny, who was crippled in one arm, were on disability.

***

Aside from Manuel, the man I remember in Duran with greatest fondness is Susano Madril. To hear him speak, you would not think he was Mexican-American. Susano was handsome with a wide face and a broad smile with good, white teeth and a lilt in his voice like that of an Anglo rancher. In his looks and smile he reminded me very much of my grandfather's tenant farmer in Ohio. There was nothing Mexican or Hispanic about Susano, except his brown skin.

Susano was a mystery to me. Susano ranched, and in all the years I knew him, he never invited me there. I do not think he invited anyone there.

I never saw him with a woman. I asked Manuel if Susano was married. Yes, Manuel said, to a Mexican woman. Since there was a big difference between Susano and the villagers—Susano had fought in World War II and had far wider and deeper experience of humanity than others in Duran—I thought I knew why he had not chosen a wife from among them or from neighboring villages, but had gone to Mexico. But why did we never see his wife with him?

I wondered also why Susano spent his days in Duran. Why

was he not out with his cattle? Didn't he check the water tanks, windmills or fence? Since there was this difference between Susano and the villagers, why did he spend his days with the old men at Ahmed's store? I never thought that this was his town and these were his people.

Susano was like the town chief, the jefe, helping the people in their problems with government bureaucracies, filling out forms for them, acting as ombudsman, making phone calls to see that they got the help they needed.

Still, Susano was a mystery.

Susano, I was told, had been in the Bataan Death March. That meant nothing to me then, except that clearly the men on the march had suffered greatly. Susano never, that first visit, mentioned it in my hearing. In those days to him I was probably just another kid in town. But years later Susano told me that he hated the Japanese, and that he and the other G.I.s had suffered so much on the march that when American bombers flew over their prison compound, they shouted joyously. They did not care whether they would be killed so long as the Japanese were killed.

Several years before Manuel married, he went periodically to Juarez in search of a wife. There were no local available women except the teenage Louisa. Whenever Manuel or some of the other local men wanted a woman, they would get in a car and drive to Juarez. Manuel talked about going to Juarez to marry one of the prostitutes. In his wallet he carried a black and white photograph of himself seated in a booth with an arm around a pretty whore. The photograph showed Manuel smiling. The girl was smiling too.

"She say she marry me," Manuel bragged. "She beautiful, no?"

"Yes."

"She say she wait for me. She come back with me."

Manuel was having trouble with his upper front teeth, and decided to have them replaced in Juarez. Andres Garcia, a friend who had a ranch in Colorado, was going to drive Manuel to Juarez. Andres wanted Manuel to come work for him in Colorado and give Manuel a better life than he had in Duran, but Manuel would never leave Duran.

Manuel told me he was going to Juarez for his teeth two days before he was to leave, and I decided I would go with them to Juarez, then go back across the border and find a warmer spot somewhere in southern Arizona. My shack was too cold.

Andres was to arrive at Manuel's trailer just after sunup. We were up well before dawn. We waited. The air outside was cold and snow was falling. Several hours passed.

"He's not coming," I told Manuel.

"He'll be here," Manuel said.

When Andres came, he drove up with Raul Sanchez, whom I had never met. We took off and arrived in El Paso around noon, parked the car and crossed the bridge over the Rio Grande into Juarez.

I had never seen anything like Juarez before—wild with bro-ken down streets and music wafting out of bars. We sauntered into a café and sat at a chipped linoleum counter. I ordered a big plate of enchiladas and pitched into them. Before long a cockroach dragged itself out from under my chili but I kept on eating.

Afterwards Manuel and Andres went to the dentist's office, where Manuel had a mold made of his teeth. The replacements would be made that same day and the next he would have his teeth pulled and the replacements implanted. I could not believe it.

While Manuel was at the dentist's having a mold made of his teeth, I wandered around Juarez. I stood admiring a carved wooden chess set in a store window and someone from the store came out and said it was a good set at a very good price. I shook my head and he lowered the price. This went on two or three more times until he named an unbelievably low price. I did not need another wooden chess set and walked off.

At a designated time I met the others. That afternoon the four of us sat in booths in one of the bars, each with a whore, all of them cute young women from outlying villages who had come to Juarez to make a living. Each bar had its own whores. This was the bar where Manuel's prostitute worked and they were together. He sat there with his arm around her shoulders. He was in heaven.

Our bar had little cribs in a patio-like area behind the barroom with an old lady at the entrance to the patio who checked the customers for venereal disease.

Afterwards Andres and Raul went their own ways. Manuel and I kept drinking all that day in other bars as they blasted Mexican music into the night. Manuel and I were sharing a hotel room. We went to the hotel and tried to sleep but could not. We decided to go a bar. Our key was attached to a big holder that I did not want to carry in my pockets. Downstairs I explained to the clerk that I wanted him to hold the key for us. He thought I was giving up the room and grabbed for it. Seeing what he was up to, I held onto it and we tugged back and forth until some of the loungers jumped up to take his side. The clerk was yelling, and the loungers were yelling and threatening us. They got the key.

Manuel was not sure what was happening. I was furious. I stomped outside followed by Manuel, and once outside raved about how we had been cheated. "We'll get some dynamite," I told him. "I'm going to blow the hotel up." I have a few scattered recollections of reeling through Juarez streets, looking for a store—maybe a hardware store—that would sell dynamite. As drunk as I was, I knew I had to be cautious to avoid arrest. I had heard what happens to gringos who are arrested and held in Mexican jails. When two policemen stopped us and asked for identification, Manuel swayed and staggered as he tried to pull out his wallet. The cops looked at mine, then his.

"You can go," they told me, "but your fren' he has to stay."

I could not believe this. "No," I said, "I'll stay with him."

If they were not going to arrest me, then maybe they would help us. "We had a hotel room." I told them the clerk stole our key and kicked us out. "Help us get our room back."

"Where's these hotel?"

I told them. After a long, noisy argument with the clerk, we got back our key and made our way upstairs.

The next day Manuel had his teeth pulled and the new ones implanted. He was in pain, and you knew it when he tried to grin. A few years later I heard that his gums had gotten terribly infected.

The next day the four of us crossed the border bridge into Texas. Nearby lay the freight yards. I got my pack from Andres' car and bid them goodbye and that night hopped a freight to Tucson where, for some reason, I began heading north instead of south. I hitched to Flagstaff, not far from the Grand Canyon. I did not know where I was going, except that I wanted to escape the cold, but could not. I was out of money. I wired home for fifty dollars from my stash but left the Western Union office before it arrived. I got back on Route 66 and hitched a ride from a trucker all the way back to Duran, where he braked in front of Ahmed's store.

Ahmed would not let me have the shack again. "You know you did wrong, leaving without telling me." Everyone else thought that was crap. Armando, the postmaster said, "What does he want you to do, kiss his ass?" Manuel offered to let me bunk with him, in his trailer, which I did for the next six weeks. By the time I left Duran in early spring, I had sunk roots into the town, and for the next twenty years I returned periodically.

After returning from Arizona, I received a letter from Sean Fitzpatrick. Sean and I had been classmates our freshman and sophomore years in high school, after which he moved with his family to Westchester County, New York, not far from New Canaan. Our parents were friends and our families visited each other periodically. Sean and I sometimes met in New York and knocked around.

Like me, Sean was an outsider. It had not always been so for Sean. Up until high school, he had been a model student. He was brilliant and by his junior year was as alienated from his town and its culture as I was from New Canaan and its culture. He was becoming increasingly cynical.

After graduating, we kept in touch. In Duran I received several letters from him. The first said he was going to a monastery and receiving instruction. He was thinking of becoming a monk. The ascetic life had appealed to me, too, but simply as an idea.

This was at a time in our lives when ideas had great force for us. We both yearned for what Sean called absolutes. These were not, of course, absolutes at all, but ideal human types. For us the foremost human types were the warrior, the saint, the poet, the philosopher. The most extreme, and therefore the most attractive for us, were the warrior and the saint. We yearned to follow, with undeviating intensity, one of these. But what were we?

In a world becoming increasingly bland—and you must remember that in our childhoods, society's constraints were becoming ever tighter—we sought authenticity. What prepared us for the search for absolutes, the ideal human types, had largely to do with our reading mythic and romantic literature. We knew the Greek and Nordic myths. We had both read Tolkein and I had read Thomas Malory and Walter Scott.

Then, after all these works and writers came *Lawrence of Arabia,* David Lean's beautiful film of T.E. Lawrence's Mideast adventures. This stunning work impelled us to read Lawrence biographies. Lawrence became for us an expression of the ideal warrior, complicated by the fact that he was also an ascetic. He was learned in mathematics and languages; he was one of the finest writers of his age; he drove us to comprehend the whole.

So, in Duran I was getting letters from Sean expressing his pain and dissatisfaction with his life in Westchester County. He was working on a survey crew, studying with a monk at a monastery, and reading Nietzsche. At the beginning of my two-month stay in Duran, Sean wanted to join the monastery, but soon Nietzsche was influencing his thinking, and the monk told Sean he was unfit for monastic life. By the end of my stay, Sean had enlisted the army with the intention of joining Special Forces.

When I received his letter in which he said he was coming to Duran, I was not pleased. Sean with his cynicism would not have fit in. Even if he could rent a room in someone's house, he would not want to spend any time with Manuel or Armando or the kids. He would have talked with Ahmed a day or two in Ahmed's general store, and then that would have grown old. He might have made my time in Duran difficult. I wrote him a letter discouraging him from coming, telling him I was not going to stay much longer.

Life in Duran was simple, too simple for Sean. It would have bored him, but it was just right for me. There was little I had to do except chop wood, buy food, wash clothes and cook. Maybe once a week Manuel and I drove from Duran to Vaughn to do our laundry. Those were the only times we went to Vaughn. Very seldom did we buy food there since Manuel, like many of Duran's residents, received government commodities. We bought what little else we needed from Ahmed.

I had given up trying to write and instead was drawing portraits of Duran residents, including the Lucero brothers. Most of the sketches I drew on a small drawing pad, but the portrait of Luis Lucero I drew on a brown bag. Luis took it home and made a frame and hung it. I drew sketches of others, including Armando and his brother, Enrique.

Life in that way moved gently. I was not bored. I was learning. Life was gentle and quiet.

The most excitement for Duran came the day a Southern Pacific freight train overturned near Vaughn. Word of the derailment spread like a rush of electric current through town. We all jumped seemingly simultaneously into pickups and roared off to Vaughn where we parked and ran to the overturned freight cars. We were not the first there. The cars had fallen onto a slight embankment over which figures were swarming.

We ran towards them. The huge doors of the refrigerator cars were open and people were handing out boxes of frozen vegetables and meats. Manuel, Benny, and I grabbed as much as we could, packing the flatbed of Manuel's truck with as much as it would hold.

This was a break. Most families in Duran received government commodities. Manuel and the others would drive to Vaughn where the monthly shipments were distributed. Each shipment contained flour, lard, potatoes, rice, tinned meat, bread, and margarine. With these commodities Manuel cooked the same dinner every day. He would slice his potatoes, heat an iron skillet, add the lard, then the potatoes. When they began sizzling he would salt and pepper the potatoes and sprinkle on red chili powder. Always he would add beef or pork cut into small pieces. With each meal we had either tortillas or white bread and coffee. Except for fried eggs and bacon and tortillas at breakfast, with an occasional orange, we ate little else.

After each meal of the day we would have a cigarette with our coffee. Usually we rolled our own cigarettes with Bull Durham tobacco, which was usually thoroughly dry and stale and not easy to roll. For me, at least, it was not easy. Unless you rolled your cigarette tight, bits of hot ash or burning tobacco would fall off and burn a hole in your shirt or pants. Manuel and I only rolled our own when we ran out of Lucky Strikes.

Sometime after dinner the kids and Benny would show up and we would sit around the small wood-burning stove in the tiny trailer. That is when I began making my drawings, mostly profiles. The talk was mostly among the kids and they spoke English as long as I was around.

One day, when I was alone in the trailer, I answered a banging on the trailer door. It was Raul Sanchez.

"Do you want to work?"

"Where?"

"The Hamra's. We need help with sheering. Bad. "

"No."

I did not need the money. I still had some from my survey job. I look back now and I cannot believe that I turned down a day or two's work that would have given me a new experience.

I left Duran at the end of March, after living there two months. One of the kids had gotten into Manuel's trailer and defaced some of my sketches by drawing earrings with a ballpoint pen on some of the portraits. I was furious. I went around town with the defaced sketches in my hand and complained to Armando and anyone else I could find.

"This is not right!" I said.

Armando agreed.

Not long after I packed my rucksack and left Duran. Manuel drove me to Vaughn where I took a bus back east.

For years I kept returning to Duran, where I would stay with Manuel at the small wood house that he bought sometime after I left in 1963. The house was grayed by rain and age, and surrounded by a wire-fenced yard. I would sit with Manuel and his neighbors, or with Manuel and the woman he married in 1970, on the battered chairs that sat outdoors. Those were quiet days, and it was good to be with humble people whose hearts were clean. Armando, the postmaster, once said, "Duran is your second home." It felt like it.

But back in 1963, on one of my walks to the edge of town at sunset I stood at the barbed wire fence that marked off the Hamra ranch. A freight car filled with hay bails sat a hundred yards beyond the fence. As I stood at the fence I heard hoof beats drumming the earth and a band of Arabian horses came galloping towards the freight car—red, pale blue, grey, gold, white—waves of horses leaping and plunging, cascading over one another.

Whatever the truth of that moment was, whatever the colors and the motions really were, it is the poetry that I remember, an image that returns unbidden, flamboyant against the prosaic landscape of the Great Plains and the ordinariness of life in Duran.

TWELVE
New York City (1964-65)

I returned from Duran in March. By June I was enrolled at Columbia University and living in Hamilton Hall, one of the large campus dormitories. There was nothing comfortable about the dorm rooms or the common room, which was dull and shabby and filled with uncomfortable furniture, as though it had been designed to keep students out.

The Columbia campus is comprised of huge brick and stone, three-story buildings without ornamentation. The library, dorms, and classroom buildings are dull-colored, utilitarian, rectangular blocks. The campus is almost entirely bare of grass. There is none of the beauty of Princeton with its graceful architecture and lawns. Columbia is as lacking in beauty as the New York subway system. It is drab. No amount of trees or plantings could ever change that. Columbia is a perfect mirror for nearly the entirety of Manhattan.

I decided to major in philosophy, not English. The discipline of philosophy would help me think clearly, besides what use could I make of an English major? Eventually I would teach myself to write, and if I could not, having majored in English would not have mattered. That summer, as it turned out, was an excellent time to enroll in introductory philosophy. The course was taught by a young man named Benson who chose A.J. Ayer's *Language, Truth, and Logic*, a classic work of twentieth-century British thought, as one of our texts.

I had no intuition of or belief in a reality beyond the here and now. And assuredly, neither did Ayer. Since Ayer asserted that any claim that could not be empirically tested was nonsense, he made perfect sense to me. To a young man eager to argue just to test his wits, Ayer's work was a perfect tool of demolition.

Benson's class was one of two in which I learned anything of value for my twelve months at Columbia. Few of my professors had a passion for their subject; most were wasting our time, certainly mine, to say nothing of my parents' money. Most professors taught mechanically. The dullest was a Chaucer class with a professor who cared nothing for the great sounds of Middle English and never read Chaucer's poetry to us dramatically. Chaucer simply seemed another cultural mummy not worth preserving. Only years later, reading *The Canterbury Tales* aloud to myself, did the scenes and characters spring to life.

Just as much a waste was a required composition class taught by an ex-advertising copywriter. I learned more about language on my own in Butler library, where I continued reading the plays of Marlowe and discovered the prose of his friend, Thomas Nashe. I could not read much of their language without feeling light-headed and would have to walk outside for my mind to settle. Their energy fired my own: their words expressed ranges of feeling, thought, and sensibility of which I had no experience, and which I yearned to grasp.

My twelve months in New York were hardly about formal education. The city itself, not Columbia, was my university. I went to jazz clubs in the Village, prowled Fourth Avenue used bookshops, saw Off-Broadway plays and studied paintings at the Frick Collection and the Metropolitan Museum of Art, but most of all at the Huntington Hartford Museum, where I marveled at Salvador Dali's epic size canvases that hung on the museum's staircase landings. Walking up the wide stairs and seeing for the first time works so complex and of such technical virtuosity I was stunned, then left reeling. I returned many times to the Dalis for a nourishment I did not find at Columbia.

High culture fed one need, scanning the lower depths of Manhattan, Times Square in particular, fed another. In those years Times Square was a tawdry area of hookers, addicts, and bars. Junkies and prostitutes argued on littered sidewalks. Times Square, dark at night and always filled with the air of decadence, fascinated me.

At that time my New Canaan schoolmate Larry Blake was living in lower Manhattan. When I think of Times Square, I think of Larry. Not that Larry haunted the square, but his wildness, his ever-on-the-edge manic-depressive, alcohol fueled life seemed to fit with Times Square.

Whenever I picture Larry I see his dark eyes and black hair and half smirk with always a cigarette dangling out of his mouth. Larry was a man of moods, swinging abruptly from high-voltage energy when his wit was incisive, to periods when hope was gone and his wit turned bitter. We both saw cracks in the world, but Larry's temperament drew him periodically into the shadows. He was a man of high intelligence, and with this intelligence and his wild humor he could have become a fine comic writer, but Larry lacked focus and concentration. Something had crippled his will and focus years before; I never knew what. Depression would overtake him and he would drink. For the remainder of his years in New York Larry jumped between marginal jobs.

One fall evening during this time Larry and I visited a bar and when we returned to his apartment I sat in an armchair facing Larry's bed. He lay there smoking. As my eyes fell shut, I wanted to tell Larry, "Put the cigarette out," but he was already asleep and I did not have the strength to talk.

I awoke to the grating sound of a smoke alarm. Smoke filled the room. Larry lay on his bed, his mattress smoldering. I stood and called, "Larry!" No answer. "Larry!" He opened his eyes. Groggy. Then came to with a start.

Suddenly I heard a banging on the apartment door. I unlocked and opened it and Larry's landlord, in white underwear, strode in.

The landlord and I drenched the sheets and mattress with water.

"Have you been drinking?" Shmmons demanded.

Larry mumbled a reply.

"You're out of here tomorrow!" Shimmons shouted. "You could have burned the building down! You're out of here!"

Perhaps I saw Larry once or twice a month in the city, and though we sometimes sat in bars, we never went together to Mc-Sorley's Old Ale House on Eighth Street on the lower East Side, an area of tenements filled with the working class, hipsters and musicians.

McSorley's had two rooms. The bar was in front—an old unpolished wooden bar a century old with sawdust on the floors and a potbelly stove in the back room. Behind the back room were a galley kitchen on one side and the men's room on the other, with an old urinal that stretched four or five feet, for a group piss.

However it was I first discovered McSorley's, I began heading to the Lower East Side on Friday or Saturday nights. This was a bar unlike any I had ever seen—a genuine workingman's bar—no women allowed. I was the youngest male there. I sat by myself for one or two visits, sharing one of the old round wooden tables with strangers.

One night, sitting at a table in the front room, I became intrigued with the conversation at the table next to me. Four men sat there, two or three with old sports jackets. In those days, as a Columbia schoolmate said, even the New York bums wore jackets. But these were not bums. I had spotted interesting men who obviously had lived. Hearing their conversation, I must have commented on something said, and someone answered me, and I asked if I could join them. For the rest of that fall and winter, whenever I was in New York for the weekend, I visited McSorley's and sat with them.

The three men I remember always sat at the same table. They had a scuffed look, a blend of Village intellectual and working class. One of the core was a hefty unpublished writer, whose last name was Reardon. Reardon, whose first name I have long forgotten, was a writer and always sat in the same chair, with his back to the wall. He was working on a novel, *Jasper*.

The second man of the trio, Mike Decker, was looking for work. The third member of the core, Earl Kravitz, was a Humphrey Bogart look-alike. Earl, like me, was a bug on Bogart's movies. Earl could be silent and morose and had been committed several times to Belleview Hospital for psychotic episodes.

I was twenty, and these men were in their fifties. A few times we left McSorley's to listen to jazz at the Blue Note. I have long forgotten our conversations, but the importance of our conversations for me was not the subjects of talk, but the fact that we did talk, and that they accepted me. The one conversation I do remember came on a winter's night. Kravitz and I were discussing Bogart movies, and in the course of it I asked if he had seen Tokyo Joe.

"Who's in it?" he asked.

"Bogart," I said.

"I never saw it," Kravitz said, rankled. Something began stirring. Earl jumped up and flung his beer at me. As soon as that beer splattered the table, McSorley's younger bartender leaped over the bar, grabbed Kravitz and hustled him out the door. Several times later that winter evening Kravitz pushed his face against McSorley's window to look at us. Not much later, he was back in Belleview.

A year after I last saw the group, I returned to McSorley's. The group was gone. I learned that Mike Decker had been hired by the Ford Foundation and no longer came to McSorley's. Kravitz had also disappeared. Reardon had died the night *Jasper* went to press. A framed dust jacket of *Jasper* still hangs on the wall behind the chair where Reardon always sat.

There was no pretence among these men. I doubt if I will meet their like again. McSorley's, of course, has changed, and is nothing like the bar it was. The women's movement killed it, and now not only women but college kids flood inside. No working-man is to be seen.

***

During spring term I developed a lung infection that forced me to return home and commute each day to the city and back with New York executives. The train was the perfect metaphor for their lives. They sat in rows, each reading a newspaper and wearing identical or nearly identical drab blue, gray, or brown suits, riding the train back and forth, back and forth, from Connecticut to New York, New York to Connecticut. Watching these corporate managers sit passively for two hours a day, reading their newspapers on the ride to and from the city, I saw no spark of animation or creative fire ever light their eyes. They made nothing, these men; they simply managed that which was not theirs.

During this period I decided to transfer back to St. John's. There had been no coherence to the Columbia experience; my classes had been unrelated. That was the university's fault as much as mine, for the School of General Studies had no core courses and no thought for the kind of person it wanted to develop, or the skills it wanted to impart.

Unlike Columbia, St. John's had a required, non-elective curriculum more rigorous than its Ivy League counterparts. St. John's knew the skills it wanted to impart. I re-applied to the college's Santa Fe campus and was admitted as a sophomore, but I chose to return as a first year student to experience as fully as I could the intellectual content of freshman studies.

PART TWO

ONE
ST. JOHN'S (1965-66)

I had never seen anything like Santa Fe before, not even in the crumbling New Mexican towns like Duran. The houses in Duran were mostly wood-frame dwellings, many boarded up. Doors and window frames were grayed from rain and cracked; chunks of plaster had fallen off walls of adobe homes. Buildings were roofed with corrugated tin, weeds grew in dirt yards.

Santa Fe was different. It had its barrios—neighborhoods where poor Hispanics lived in adobes surrounded by dirt yards—but it also had sections of small, well-kept middle-class houses surrounded by low adobe walls. Santa Fe also had a small population of the rich, who in those days were not conspicuous.

St. John's, sitting in the foothills of the Sangre de Cristo mountains, overlooked Santa Fe. The land and hills were covered with piñons and junipers. Not much else besides the juniper and piñons grew on the landscape except scattered clumps of grass and sage and low-growing cactus that clung to the earth.

Beyond the campus the hills folded into mountains that seemed to roll on forever. The air was clean and there was great clarity to the light.

I immediately dug into my studies with a diligence that surprised myself.

Mac Johnson was also a freshman, a twenty-four-year-old man of unrestrained energy exuberantly yelling a great hello to life—a striking counterpart to the my Columbia acquaintances who were preparing for careers in business and finance. Now I was suddenly thrown face to face with a young man almost my opposite, one with no intellectual pretensions but great physical strength.

Mac said what he thought, laughed loudly and often. He had an enormous appetite for food and beer, and a curiosity for how things worked. Thanks to Mac what I got out of Santa Fe that year was less about books and ideas than experience of people.

Mac had never graduated from high school, but nevertheless had briefly attended other colleges before St. John's, where he was diagnosed with dyslexia. He wanted very much to master the great books, but his mind was geared for creativity and mechanical invention: it was original, not designed for the ruts of academia.

But as Mac tried to study, frustration would overcome him, or a desire to run, to talk, to explore. Santa Fe with its clean mountain air, its light, its adobe architecture and its mix of Hispanic, Indian, and Anglo cultures offered a new angle of being. So that while I studied and Mac tried to study, we thought of all that beckoned to us, and we went—to bars, restaurants, and artists' studios. We took long drives to towns made of baked mud and straw, pitched on the sides of mountains. Rutted dirt roads wound between houses that seemed about to slide down mountain slopes. These towns with winding streets and mud-baked homes seemed medieval or Moroccan—secretive and foreboding. Unfriendly eyes stared as we passed.

We spent long hours cruising through Santa Fe in Mac's 1961 Mercedes. Its body was rusted, its exhaust pipes had fallen off, its leather upholstery was worn and faded. Mac had bolted wooden beams to its front and rear bumpers. When I asked why, he said, "To protect them."

I drove the Mercedes downtown many times. I felt good driving it. Sitting behind its wheel I acquired the ability to size the world from an eccentric angle and lived as I should, without fear, as Mac did.

Soon after winter break I met Alan Hays. I had entered the building that housed the library when I glanced inside. I saw a man sitting at a table; for some reason I stopped. I looked at him and he looked up, at me. He had a high forehead, a mustache, and deep-set, intelligent eyes. I felt I knew him and he must have felt that he knew me. He stood and waved—tentatively—and I waved back. There was an awkward pause before I walked on. Later, as I thought about him I remembered seeing a man three years earlier on the Annapolis campus who looked like him.

A few days later at noon I saw Alan in the dining hall. Mac was with me. I said, "Let's sit over there," nodding with my head. "I want to meet the tall guy."

We walked to Alan and introduced ourselves. We learned that Alan had served three years with the army in Alaska and was now married with two young boys. He had been supporting his wife Gail and their children, or trying to support them, by teaching piano, but Gail was now at her mother's with the boys. Alan, at twenty-seven, was returning to St. John's as a freshman. Far from being dim, he was possibly the most intelligent person on campus.

Winter snow was melting the afternoon Alan rushed into our dorm and announced to Mac and me that he had discovered a great painter. He sat down on the edge of Mac's bed. "He's as good as Van Gogh. You've got to see him."

He drove us down the hill to Canyon Road and parked in front of a one-story stuccoed house. A hand-painted sign above the front door read:

PAINTINGS
Tommy Macaione—El Differente

El Differente had a painting propped in his window, an intense landscape reminiscent of Van Gogh.

We jumped out of the car. Alan knocked on the screen door and Tommy called, "Wait! Wait!" Moments later he pulled the door open, and through the screen said, "I can't let you in yet. I can't let my babies out." He pushed his dogs aside with his feet, all the while talking loudly to them. We entered a tiny living room empty of furniture but stacked with paintings. The paintings were in various stages of completion. They were painted with thick daubs and streaks of color, wild profusions of emotion. But on one wall he hung two conventionally rendered paintings—one of a pair of flamenco dancers, another of a pipe and a bowl with fruit. "I hang those," Tommy said, "so that people will know that I can paint like that, if that's what they want."

A stench filled the room. Tommy's clothes were covered with dog hair. His bed was covered with dog hair, the sheets and cover balled together. Empty dog food cans with bits of decayed meat lay on the floor next to dog turds. There were wet spots and stains where his dogs had peed.

Tommy had the title "El Differente" legally affixed to his

name. And different he was. He was in his mid-fifties with a long unkempt beard, hideous breath, and hair that shot out in all directions. He was missing several teeth; those he had were brown and yellow.

"I'm having a terrible time," Tommy told us, "I'm STARVING. Things are worse, Alan. I passed out just the other day and the day before that, too, I'm so hungry. I haven't enough to even feed my babies."

His eyes watered and he spoke frantically, in a rush.

"We can help you out, Tommy," Alan told him. "How about coming up to dinner this evening?"

"Boys, do you mean it?"

"Sure we do," Alan said.

"I love you boys," he said, grabbing Alan and hugging him. "Can you drive me downtown? Do you have time? I have to get some bones for my dogs, they're starving. God would be very angry with me if I let them die."

"Sure," Alan said, "let's get in the car."

Tommy sat up front with Alan. His smell sickened me. Mac and I rolled down our windows but the rush of air could not eliminate his odor.

We drove to a grocery store where Tommy walked to the meat department and returned with large bags filled with bones and meat scraps. Meanwhile, I bought a box of spaghetti, several cans of tomato sauce, Italian sausage, two loaves of bread, and a can of soup.

"This ought to hold you for a while," I told him.

He cried and hugged me.

I was happy for him and envious of his intensity and dedication and lack of inhibition, but his sentimentality embarrassed me.

That night Alan brought him to the dining room, a large hall with balconies and clean light wood tables. The hall was clean, spare, modern. Tommy wore a torn corduroy coat with bulging pockets, baggy pants thinning at the knees, and old cracked shoes with knotted laces. With his wild hair and unkempt beard Tommy looked as out of place as anyone could. But we were proud of our find; after all, we were mingling with the townspeople.

That struck me as the big gap between us and the other students: they had little to do with the town. Their interests were in the program, themselves, and a handful of friends. We, on the other hand, lived only partly for St. John's. You might say the books were for us a jumping off point, a different way of exploring the world, a kind of background to it. The real thing was life, people.

"God bless you boys, God bless you," Tommy kept saying.

When Kyle our waiter told us the selections, Tommy said excitedly, "You mean I can have a choice?"

Alan said, "Sure. And if you want more later you can have it."

When Kyle brought our orders Tommy immediately pitched into his food, gobbling it and talking while he ate. "St. John's is a great school, a great school. You boys are very lucky to be here. Me, I didn't have a college education. I went to art school. I knew very early I wanted to be a painter."

"Have you always made your living as a painter?" I asked.

"A living!" he practically screamed. "I can't make a living at painting now!"

"Right," I said.

"I was a barber for years, in New York. When I came to Santa Fe in fifty-three I was a barber."

His fingers were greasy from picking up food with his hands. When bits of meat and vegetables became entangled in his beard, he did not notice.

"If you boys want to do me a favor," he said loudly, his mouth filled with food, "something God will bless you for, get me a show at St. John's."

"All right" Alan said, "we'll do that."

Periodically the college hung an art exhibit in a gallery on the balcony overlooking the dining hall. We arranged Tommy's show through Colonel Deal, who curated the exhibits. We arranged to meet Colonel Deal at Tommy's studio. Colonel Deal brought his station wagon and selected the paintings and we stacked them in his car and in Mac's. We spent the afternoon hanging the show while Tommy walked around, jabbering excitedly, "God will bless you. I pray for you. You are good boys for doing an old man this kindness."

We had Tommy to dinner several more times. For fifteen years Tommy had starved in Santa Fe. Whenever things got especially tough he took out a large ad in *The Santa Fe New Mexican*—the town paper—pleading for help. He traded paintings for the ads. Now he thought his fortunes were changing. He thought that with a show at St. John's he would begin to attract wealthy buyers. He wrote prices of three and five hundred dollars on small cards in a scrawl and posted them next to the paintings. Then he scratched out those prices and scribbled in higher ones.

For days afterwards we spent hours with Tommy in Mac's room before a tape recorder as he told us his life story and his theories of art. He wrote huge summaries of these in his large hand on greasy papers. All this was for a biography and artist's statement, which we were to type up and photocopy and put in a stack in the gallery. We never wrote the biography or the statement. Tommy kept walking or hitchhiking up to St. John's to see the show. Benevolence and gratitude changed to indignation. He railed at us.

"For two months now you've done nothing," he would say. "That's not right. You made a promise and if you're gentlemen you're supposed to stick to them."

He was right.

Tommy painted outdoors around Santa Fe in all weather. I remember his large paintings of hollyhocks that grew in profusion along Santa Fe sidewalks. Tommy was most interested in flowers, shrubs, and bushes, sometimes set against houses. In winter he wore several corduroy jackets and torn trousers, painting outside on the bitterest days. I saw him painting one evening at dusk to catch the last of the flowers before the autumn frost. When Tommy was not painting or begging scraps for his dogs, he would walk all five of his pets, getting the dogs and himself entangled as they dragged him across Santa Fe.

***

Mac, Alan, and I with two other friends founded a dining club that met in the president's dining room, on one side of the dining hall.

We held our dinners Friday nights and I began inviting interesting Santa Feans. Besides Tommy Macaione, one of our guests
was Jack Schaefer, the author of *Shane*. It was through Jack Schaefer that I learned of the West family. Schaefer told us: "There's
Hal West the artist. He's got four sons, each of them different.
One's a rancher, one's a painter, one's an insurance salesman, the
fourth does I don't know what. Then there's Hal's brother Gene,
the rancher." After hearing that, I wanted to meet the Wests, especially Hal and Archie, both of whom Schaefer described enthusi-
astically.

TWO
Hal and Friends

When the college year ended, Mac and I moved into an old hotel
in Cerrillos. We were staying at the hotel because Mac, Alan, I and
another friend had the idea of starting a summer camp there. Actually, it was Alan's idea. The hotel owner, who did not have money,
needed a way to restore the hotel. With money from one of us we
bought supplies and began repainting the upstairs in exchange for
rent. All of us except our friend the investor quit when it was clear
we did not have the money to open the camp.

Mac and I had returned to Santa Fe and threw our blankets
on the floor of Alan's home on Canyon Road. Alan's rental was
across the street from Hal West's studio. I remembered well Jack
Schaefer's words about the Wests, especially about Hal. I wanted
to meet him. I was sitting on a wicker rocker on Alan's front porch
on a morning when Hal opened his door to collect his newspaper.
Alan stepped outside his house and called, "Hello, Hal West!"

Hal said, "Morning, kiddo," and stepped back inside. I walked
across the road to meet Hal, and when Mac and Alan arrived later,
Hal invited us to play dominoes. We were enjoying the game, trying to block each other from playing. It was fun and we were
laughing whenever someone had to pick among the bone pile for
a domino to play. But a peculiar thing happened. Mac made a

smart aleck comment to Hal like, "Come on, come on, don't take so long thinking about what you're gonna play. Make your move," and we noticed that Hal was just sitting rigidly, staring at Mac. We said nothing but looked at one another. We thought Hal was mad at Mac, but soon realized that was not the problem.

"Hal!" Alan called.

Hal did not move.

"Hal!" he called again.

Hal, still staring, opened his mouth and ran his tongue along his lips. His eyes were vacant; he dropped his cigarette on the floor. Alan picked it up. Finally Hal's eyes focused and he cleared his throat. "Whose move is it?" he asked.

I had seen Hal's bare refrigerator and was sure that Hal had had this episode from lack of food. "Listen," I said, "I'll go get some food. You fellows stay here."

"Where you going?" Hal asked. He seemed puzzled and unfocused.

"You need some food. I'll be back in a minute."

I went to Percy's, a small grocery store fifty paces from Hal's. When I returned with a small bag of food it was evident that Hal was normal again, and from the talk it appeared that he was not undernourished. I put the groceries in the refrigerator.

Hal said, "Kid, you didn't have to do that."

"Well, you didn't have much in here."

We went back to playing dominoes, with no mention of Hal's episode. Mac and Alan were not talking about it, and in the two years I knew Hal he never talked about it either. What it was, I later found out, was a petit mal, a seizure of sorts, lasting almost ten minutes. People tried to explain it with two stories. Some said that as a boy Hal had worked on a Mississippi riverboat and had gotten into an argument with the fireman over a poker game. The fireman ran out and came back with a shovel and cracked Hal on the side of the head. Others said that Hal had had a rotten upper molar. A dentist had extracted it, but had failed to get the roots, which caused an infection that eventually went into Hal's brain. A tumor developed and Hal traveled to Chicago for surgery. Everyone thought he would die. Hal never mentioned the tumor afterwards, but referred to trouble in the head, the dentist, and the decayed tooth. The dentist was someone he very much hated.

***

Pete Townsend, an ex-adman who I met through Hal used to say, "We had a big way of living then." Townsend got that line from A. B. Guthrie's novel, *The Big Sky* and he meant that he and his friends, perhaps all of Santa Fe, had once upon a time lived lives fit for legend. But Santa Fe was not that way at all, not at least in the mid-sixties when I arrived. The days of big living had vanished over a century before, when Santa Fe was just a dusty village, one of the northernmost outposts of Mexico, inhabited mostly by Mexicans along with a handful of Indians and traders. In those days Santa Fe was a lot quieter than Taos, ninety miles to the north. The fur traders and mountain men headquartered in Taos, closer to the high country with the beaver and the streams that curled down from the heights. Taos, the center of the American fur trade, was a wild town of mountain men, trappers, Indians and Mexicans. If any place in New Mexico had a big way of living, it was Taos.

As I came to know later, I arrived in the last decade of what remained of Santa Fe's intensely creative period. That period began in the first half of the twentieth century when the city and surrounding country attracted great artists and photographers, as well as characters. What experience I gleaned from what remained of earlier decades I got from Hal and his friends who dropped by for a cup of coffee and a game of dominoes. Looking back, these meetings with Hal's friends were the beginning of my Santa Fe education—in people and in ways of being that are no longer.

Hal was a man of an older time, of a culture gone decades before. By the fact that in his last years Hal was quiet and slow to move—not lethargic—he embodied for me a sense of time or timelessness that must have been characteristic of Santa Fe years before. In Hal's studio I was immersed in an older America. It was there on the walls of Hal's kitchen: photos of Burro Alley in 1920s downtown Santa Fe where woodcutters came down from the mountains with their burros loaded with firewood for sale. There were burros hitched to tie racks in one, and in another, burros lay in the dirt street next to adobes. There were also photos of Hal and friends at Hal's legendary poker parties that were no more.

Hal had a bit of actor in him. He called ladies "ma'm" and complained about the short length of dresses and the women who wore shorts. Short dresses and women's shorts were special objects of disdain. In fact, when a woman with shorts came into the studio he would tell her to go home and change clothes. I had heard about this from others before I saw it for myself the afternoon a small cluster of women wearing shorts walked into the studio and began looking at the paintings. Without getting out of his kitchen chair Hal told them from the kitchen, "Go home and get a dress on. I don't want women with shorts in here. When you get a dress on then you'll be welcome back."

"Are you serious?"

"Yes, I am."

Another favorite topic was the effeminacy of businessmen. Hal considered businessmen effeminate, I think, because they were not working men, earning a living plastering, or picking cotton, or cowboying. Hal's experience of businessmen was limited to Santa Fe shopkeepers. He had no experience of aggressive corporate managers.

Harking back to an earlier America, Hal extolled the virtues of bourbon, "pore ole boys" and old-fashioned women.

***

Hal came to our melodrama the day we met and returned to Santa Fe that night with Mac and Alan. The next day Mac said, "Hal told us about his brother Gene, a rancher. When we were driving along Cerrillos Road he pointed to a bar and said his brother had cleared it out." Mac laughed. "He said his brother's real wild." Right then I wanted to meet Gene.

I returned to Hal's studio every day for the next month, arriving each morning as soon as he placed the "open" sign on his screen door. We would begin the day with eggs and potatoes fried with scraps from the night before, downed with day old bitter coffee.

After the first few days I asked Hal if I could bring my typewriter over. Of course I could, and that morning—and for many others—I went to the back room with my typewriter where I drummed out stories of my road trips on long sheets of brown wrapping paper that I cut into strips.

Most afternoons I sat and listened to Hal unroll stories of his boyhood in Tishomingo, Oklahoma, where he chopped cotton and paid no mind to school lessons, and instead sketched classmates. Hal told me stories of Depression days spent wandering the country, hitchhiking and on foot. He talked of walking through the Ozarks, trying to thumb a ride. "I'd pass by houses with people sitting on their porches and they would call out to me and get to talking, asking me where I was from and where I was going. People were friendly and curious in those days, not like now."

During the Depression years Hal visited Santa Fe. In New York, at a Greenwich Village party he told other artists about Santa Fe, then looked out an apartment window to the backs of sooty tenements and said, "Boys, tomorrow I'm heading for Santa Fe." Others there said they would follow him.

On his way back to Santa Fe, Hal stopped in Ohio to woo a young woman he had met on his way east. They were married and Hal found work in Ohio, and stayed six months before continuing west. When he arrived in Santa Fe, his artist friends had already settled there.

Later, during World War II, Hal worked as a guard at a Japanese internment camp outside Santa Fe. In a sketch of the camp Hal showed his feet propped on a railing, with buildings in the background. Some years after the war Hal bought a homestead on the Cerrillos flats, about twenty miles from Santa Fe, where he and his wife, Mildred, raised four boys and a girl.

These were some of the stories Hal told in the afternoons as we sat together, drinking coffee.

***

When I entered his studio one day Hal told me, "There's a very nice young gal that came by earlier today. She'll be back this afternoon. You'll like her."

Shortly afterwards, the young woman arrived.

"Bob," Hal said, "I want you to meet Lillian Payne, a very nice gal from New York."

Lillian and I shook hands. Lillian was several years older than I with a face that was pleasant but not intelligent. Lillian wore a colorful, billowy blouse and a long skirt. From Lillian and Hal's expressions it was clear that Hal was very pleased with Lillian, and she was entranced with him. Lillian told me she was a secretary in New York and was here on vacation and staying at La Fonda. Lillian was pleasant and smiled easily.

When she excused herself to use Hal's bathroom, Hal said, "That gal would make you a good wife." I knew Hal well enough to know why he said that. Lillian wore long skirts and was pleasant and was not likely to challenge a man.

As the three of us talked, Hal's back door opened and a man called, "Harold, how are you?"

A tall, lean man in jeans and western hat stepped inside. The man stooped slightly and spoke slowly. He seemed worn and tired.

"I'm getting on, Gene. I want you to meet two young friends of mine. The young fella sitting there is Bob Wolf. And this nice young gal is Lillian Payne."

I stood and Gene and I shook hands

In a moment the phone rang and Harold went to the other room to answer it. I had forgotten that the man who now seated himself on a bench against a wall was the man that Mac said had cleared out a bar not long before.

I asked, "Gene, what do you do?"

"I have a little piece of land south of here. I raise cattle."

I was interested. "Could you use an extra hand?" I asked.

"Bob, I've got enough trouble just supporting my family. I'm barely hanging on. The ranch doesn't keep us. I've even got to do a little building on the side to make ends meet."

After Gene left I gave no thought to seeing him again. An opportunity had been missed to know someone who was probably a quintessential American type.

Hal said, "Let's take a walk downtown."

For the next four days I saw Lillian in the late afternoons and evenings when she and I and Hal would stroll downtown for toddies at La Fonda or the Palace.

The afternoon Lillian was to leave for New York, I walked her downtown to the bus station. I necked with her in front of her bus, trying to get her to put off leaving but her mind was made up. A week later both Hal and I get letters from Lillian, which we never answered.

THREE

Marlene I (summer 1966)

Every few days Hal would mention Marlene, a friend from Texas whom he first met when she stopped in his gallery on her first trip to Santa Fe. Since then she had returned several times and their acquaintance had ripened into friendship. Every once in awhile he would mention that she had telephoned, and judging by how often he mentioned her, and by his enthusiasm, I knew she was one of the important people in his life. I was curious to meet her.

Then one day Hal said to Mac and me, "Marlene'll be coming to town pretty soon."

"Who's Marlene?" Mac asked.

"She's a good ole Texas gal. A friend of mine," he said. "She's very good to me. Brings me cakes, pies, milk, beef, whiskey. Anything I want." He grinned mischievously. "You wait and see, she'll show up soon. She's going through a divorce right now, but as soon as that clears up, she'll be out."

Hal did not mention her age, her looks, what she did, nothing except she was "a good ole gal," "jolly and generous" and "liked a good time." Judging from that, I thought she was in her thirties. And for some reason I imagined she was good looking.

A week later, as Hal, Mac, Alan, and I sat around the kitchen table playing dominoes, the back door opened and we heard a loud booming laugh that seemed to keep ringing, and in stepped a woman with curly black hair, a pointy nose, clear plastic glasses, and a big toothy grin. We turned as she bawled, "Hal West, you OLD SON OF A GUN! How are you?"

Hal's mouth dropped open, then broke into a grin. He said, "Well I'll be. Marlene. It's good to see you." He leaned forward and pushed himself up as she came at him, arms spread wide. She gave him a hug and then laid her hands on his shoulders and said, "Hal West, you're a sight for sore eyes."

"Well, God bless you, Marlene, it's good to see you," Hal said in quiet, affectionate tones.

"How've you been?" she boomed.

I did not like her looks. She annoyed me. She had interrupted our game.

"Pretty fair," Hal responded. "My health's good, knock on wood," and he rapped the table. "How've you been?"

"Oh, just fine. In fact, I'm feeling great!"

She was all smiles. Apparently the divorce had done her all the good in the world.

"Marlene," Hal said, "I want you to meet some friends." He swung round to us. "They're not worth a damn, but they're good ole boys."

We laughed and stood up. Alan, effusive as usual, stuck out an arm and pumped her hand. His voice, loud without modulation, crackled, "Pleased to meet you. We've heard a lot about you." He was always eager to create a good impression.

"Hal," she said, "I've got groceries in the car. Would one of you men," turning to us, "be kind enough to bring them in?"

"Sure," Alan and I said, and she handed us the keys. We brought back three grocery bags filled with polish sausages, bread, eggs, milk, ground beef, coffee, beans, and butter. And a fifth of Jim Beam.

Hal, delighted, called out, "This calls for a celebration! Boys, get us some glasses. And get us an extra chair."

We got the chair and glasses, opened the bottle and poured the whiskey.

"I want mine with a little branch water," Marlene said.

Alan got the "branch water" from the sink and handed the glasses round.

Marlene Jeffries, the sweetest and most generous gal in . . . shall I say Texas or New Mexico?"

"New Mexico."

"Hallelujah!"

We all drank a toast and sat down to a game of dominoes and played all that afternoon. When it was time to leave for Cerrillos, we told Marlene about the melodramas and asked if she and Hal would like to come along and she said, "A real melodrama! How wonderful! Oh, how exciting!"

***

By midsummer I was seeing less of Mac and Alan. Mac now had a small cottage on Upper Canyon Road and spent much of his time roaming Santa Fe. Alan was gone days, too, working at the Navaho Museum of Ceremonial Art. I was still spending my days at Hal's studio and my night's at Alan's.

Our drives to the melodramas continued. Those were the only times we saw Marlene, who came to every show. Now that Mac's fiancée, Mary, was in town, Mac and she drove together. Hal, Marlene, Alan and I rode together in Marlene's ostentatious car. After the first evening she became a regular at the melodramas. She learned the lines just as Hal had and would shout them out and talk back to us. But her enthusiasm was self-conscious and irritating. After the melodrama Mac and Mary would drive back to Mac's cottage while the rest of us cruised into downtown Santa Fe to the Palace Restaurant where we drank and sang, with Marlene's voice booming above all others.

One day as we sat at the kitchen table, Hal announced to Mac and me, "Brother Gene is having a branding this Wednesday. I haven't been to his place in awhile. Do you care to go?"

"Sure," we said, and Wednesday afternoon Hal, Marlene, Mac and I piled into Marlene's car and roared off towards Cerrillos. We drove several miles down the Cerrillos highway before turning onto a cattle guard and driving miles over a rutted dirt road. Finally a ranch house came into view, tucked into the back of a hill. A windmill stood on top of the rise. The house was partially surrounded by a pole stockade built to keep cattle out. We

"Gentlemen," Hal said, raising his drink, "I propose a toast to Marlene Jeffries, the sweetest and most generous gal in . . . shall I say Texas or New Mexico?"

"New Mexico."

"Hallelujah!"

We all drank a toast and sat down to a game of dominoes and played all that afternoon. When it was time to leave for Cerrillos, we told Marlene about the melodramas and asked if she and Hal would like to come along and she said, "A real melodrama! How wonderful! Oh, how exciting!"

***

By midsummer I was seeing less of Mac and Alan. Mac now had a small cottage on Upper Canyon Road and spent much of his time roaming Santa Fe. Alan was gone days, too, working at the Navaho Museum of Ceremonial Art. I was still spending my days at Hal's studio and my night's at Alan's.

Our drives to the melodramas continued. Those were the only times we saw Marlene, who came to every show. Now that Mac's fiancée, Mary, was in town, Mac and she drove together. Hal, Marlene, Alan and I rode together in Marlene's ostentatious car. After the first evening she became a regular at the melodramas. She learned the lines just as Hal had and would shout them out and talk back to us. But her enthusiasm was self-conscious and irritating. After the melodrama Mac and Mary would drive back to Mac's cottage while the rest of us cruised into downtown Santa Fe to the Palace Restaurant where we drank and sang, with Marlene's voice booming above all others.

One day as we sat at the kitchen table, Hal announced to Mac and me, "Brother Gene is having a branding this Wednesday. I haven't been to his place in awhile. Do you care to go?"

"Sure," we said, and Wednesday afternoon Hal, Marlene, Mac and I piled into Marlene's car and roared off towards Cerrillos. We drove several miles down the Cerrillos highway before turning onto a cattle guard and driving miles over a rutted dirt road. Finally a ranch house came into view, tucked into the back of a hill. A windmill stood on top of the rise. The house was partially surrounded by a pole stockade built to keep cattle out. We drove through an open gate with the house on one side and a corral opposite. Dust rose in the corral as cattle milled.

I helped Hal out of the car. As soon as he straightened, a young woman's screechy voice yelled, "Uncle Harold!" The cowboys, momentarily diverted, looked in our direction. We ambled over to the corral. A voice yelled, "Get 'im, Leon!" as a cowboy threw a rope, missed, and a calf shot away.

I spotted Gene right off. I recognized Leon because he was the one who had thrown the lasso. The other cowboy I gathered was Tom, as Gene would call out, "Get that one, Tom," and the young man would spur his horse. In a corner of the corral sat two oil drums with smoke curling out and two women standing nearby, dressed in jeans with western shirts and hats. The one who had screeched at Harold now climbed over the corral fence and ran towards us yelling, "Uncle Harold, how are you?" and flung her arms around him, giving him a big squeeze.

"Good to see you, Susie," Hal said and introduced her to us. Susie was Gene's youngest daughter, blonde and good looking. Whenever she talked, she seemed to shout. She led us to the corral gate and Hal exchanged hellos with another daughter, Margaret, taller than Susie and a real rawboned redhead with fine chiseled features and freckles.

As the three riders took turns going after calves, one of them would coil his lariat and ride around until he spotted a calf that had not been branded, spur his horse into a trot and begin swinging the rope above his head. If the calf did not disappear into the herd, he threw the rope. Most times the lariat just hit the ground, but when it hit the animal, it usually slapped against its back. Once or twice they caught a calf around the neck, but most often they snagged it when the lasso landed on the ground and one of the calf's rear feet stepped into the loop and they jerked the rope.

With the calf roped, the roper would direct his horse to the barrels, dragging the calf behind him. Susie would sit and hold the calf's front legs while a cowboy sat, pushing one of his boots against the bottom rear leg of the calf and gripping the top leg, pulling it towards him. If it was a bull calf, Gene would come with a knife, cut open its scrotum with a slash, pull out the testicles as the animal bawled and blood poured out. Then he would dip his hand into a jar of salve and smear it over the empty scrotum and Margaret would vaccinate the animal. Someone else would come with a branding iron and push it against the hide. The calf would bawl, the hide would sizzle, but when they let it go, the calf would scamper off as if nothing had happened.

At one point, when the riders were going for a particularly large calf and failed to lasso it, Mac dashed into the center of the corral. I thought, "He can't get him, that calf's too big," but Gene yelled, "Get him!" Mac actually outran the calf as it tried dodging back into the herd, grabbing hold of it with one hand around its neck, the other over its back, grasping a rear leg. He heaved the two hundred pound animal upward on its side. As it crashed to the earth, the cowboys gave a shout.

When the branding was over they let the cattle out of the corral and walked to the house, a one-story adobe shaped like a square C. The porch ran the inside the C on three sides with a bed of red and white hyacinths in the center.

Gene ambled up to a door and called, "Genie! Darlin'! We got 'er done!" and turning to the rest of us, said, "Hal, take a chair." Pulling open the door, he went inside. Soon he reappeared with a short plumpish woman with a genial face.

Hal said, "Genie, good to see you. You'll excuse me if I don't get up."

"Oh, Hal," she said, "you're excused."

Gene and Genie brought a bottle of bourbon, glasses, and a pitcher of water. We sat on the cement slab and drank, and while the others talked I listened. I had never met a family like the Wests. I could see they had a sophistication and worldliness about them but also a rawness and energy. They were the first representatives of the class of southwestern ranchers and rural Anglo peoples with whom I was later to spend much time. Their rawness, the drama that surrounded their lives, impacted me then as no other people have.

***

I was now living, day and night, among adults. The girls from St. John's were gone for the summer and I knew no place in Santa Fe where people my age mixed. Besides, I wanted to spend my time with Hal and his friends and, except for Mac and Alan, I had no desire to socialize with people my age. But, as Henry Adams might have asked himself in similar circumstance, what education did I derive from Santa Fe that summer? I was receiving an education in human types and behaviors, watching, listening, and talking to people of a kind I would never see again.

It now seems inevitable that in that summer of 1966, given the need for a sexual outlet and Marlene's oversexed nature and our drinking, that I would end up coupling with her.

I am certain that Marlene had another reason for coming to the melodrama other than watching the show. The seduction came in the back seat of her car as Alan drove us home one night. Hal sat in front seat beside him. How the seduction happened is too embarrassing to tell. Nothing outrageous was done, but an understanding was achieved, and I came to live with Marlene for the month of August.

At about this time Alan's wife Gail arrived from Austin with their two young boys. Gail was a blonde, attractive woman but harassed. According to Alan, Gail's mother was very neurotic and whenever Gail went home to her mother she returned in a foul mood. At that time Alan was working for a little over minimum wage. At twenty-seven he was still a student. At home he studied philosophy, logic and mathematics and left the house cleaning, childcare, laundry and cooking to Gail.

At this time Mac was studying Greek, preparing for a test at the end of summer. If he passed, he could remain at St. John's. Mac spent his days taking long walks in arroyos on the north edge of town while memorizing Greek vocabulary.

Though my nights were now spent with Marlene, I still spent afternoons with Hal. At Marlene's, small irritations began to build up. The toilet seat and tank were covered in green shag material. At first sight I was stunned then disgusted at seeing her attempt to sanitize a basic animal function.

Everywhere we went we took her car. Marlene never walked.

Consequently, whenever she did walk, even two blocks, she would gasp for air and have to sit down, complaining that her thighs ached from the "exercise."

In the evenings we sat around her house and drank. She drank one bourbon and water after another, and I kept up with her. We would start drinking around five o'clock and sip steadily for six hours.

There was nothing to fill the evenings except alcohol, television, and Marlene's interest in the occult. If she wanted to know the future, she would pull her ouija board from a closet, put it on her knees and speak in a low, sensuous tone, as though she were being serviced.

"Oh ouija, speak to me. Speak to me, ouija."

Through the board she was trying to connect with a spirit. She was sure the spirit would answer her questions. She put both hands on a small piece of wood. When the spirit spoke to her, it would lead her hands around the board, which was inscribed with the letters of the alphabet, the numbers 0-9 and the words "yes" and "no."

"Ouija, speak to me," she would moan.

It was hard to listen to that.

Of course the spirit always spoke to her. The spirit, though, needed prompting, because Marlene had to tilt the board with her knees to get the letters and finally the answer she wanted.

The daily horoscopes in *The New Mexican* also gave her answers and advice.

The worst part of each night came when Marlene slipped into a one or two-piece silk nightgown with wild patterns and sit on the sofa while we watched television. Eventually I would get drunk enough and horny enough to put a hand on her thigh, but I got sicker of myself every day.

Some evenings Marlene would have Alan, Gail, and the kids over for dinner and Marlene would cook big steaks. Alan, Marlene, and I would get smashed on bourbon and the kids would run havoc around the house. Marlene would pretend nothing was happening and Gail would be going quietly crazy.

Not long after seeing the movie, *Dr. Zhivago*, Alan and one of his sons sat with Marlene and I in a back booth of the Plaza Bar. I went to the jukebox and put on the theme from *Dr. Zhivago*. As I slid back into the booth, Marlene took my hand and whispered in my ear, "Thank you, darling," as though I had played it because it was "our song." I could not look at her.

One night after the melodrama I was getting tanked up as usual, this time standing at the Tiffany bar, talking with one of our actresses who smiled coyly and said, "Who's your girlfriend?" I said, "I don't have a girlfriend," and she said, "I know. Your girlfriend is Marlene." I blushed and said, "Are you kidding?"

One evening, as we drove home from the melodrama with Hal and Alan in front, Marlene and I sat in back, holding hands, Hal said, "Can't you wait till later to hold hands?" That sent me through the floor. Hal had been facing forward the entire trip. Marlene laughed and said, "Why, Hal, you shouldn't look," and Hal said, "There are a lot of things I see."

Nevertheless, I still spent afternoons at his studio, but our visits became quieter as we said less to each other. Finally one day Hal looked at me and said, "There's something peculiar about a fellow who just sits around another man's home all the time" and stared at me. I was angry and hurt, too naive to know why he said it. I stood up and said, "All right, I'll see you," and headed out the back door, intending never to return.

FOUR
Marlene II (summer 1966)

During this time Marlene was having doubts about Hal. A month or so earlier Hal had told me that Marlene had proposed to him over dinner at La Fonda. Her story was different. He, she said, had proposed to her. Now she talked a lot about Hal. "He's getting downright obnoxious," she said once. "Why he called me up this afternoon and asked to take me out to dinner. We've gone out many times and only twice did he pay the bill. He's just using me."

At first I did not pay attention to these complaints, but as she repeated them daily, I grew suspicious. She was certain that any reference Hal made to food was a suggestion that she buy him groceries. Soon my faith in Hal's integrity began eroding. I had visions of Hal conning women for the past forty years. After all, he had told me several times, "I've had the pick of the women." I now saw him sitting in his chair, wondering which woman to call next.

About mid-August Mac drove me to Marlene's after he and I had had a night at the bars. I went in through the garage into her bedroom, whispering. Her lights were out and I did not want to scare her. I undressed and got into bed beside her. We talked a while. She was afraid. She was expecting her sister-in-law early next morning and did not want me to spend the night. She pleaded with me to go. Finally I dressed and walked out, down Canyon Road to Hal's. It was a long walk on a cold night.

Hal's light was out. I hated waking him but knocked on the front door. I waited but heard nothing. I knocked again. I called out, "Hal." Then I heard a noise. It must have been Hal getting out of bed. Then I heard a BAM. I did not know what it was. I was getting impatient. "HAL!" I called out again. I heard his muffled voice say, "Wait," and heard him shuffling to the door. He opened it slowly, and I went inside.

"I fell down," he said.

"Oh," I said. "Are you all right?"

I thought he had fallen because he was sleepy or could not see in the dark.

"Just a little sore," he said quietly.

"Can I stay here the night?"

"If you want."

I got into bed next to him.

The next morning Hal felt terribly. He had a pain in his chest. He took three steps to the kitchen and leaned against the doorjamb and asked help getting to the bathroom. When he came out, I supported him as he shuffled to a kitchen chair. I called Marlene, then Hal's son, Jerry, and then Alan.

Marlene soon arrived and I put an arm around Hal and got him in her car. We drove to the hospital where Alan and I took him into the emergency room. Hal had had a stroke.

Later, Marlene said, "I knew something was wrong last night. I had a premonition. That's why I wanted you to go to Hal's."

Had she forgotten about her sister-in-law?

The next afternoon Hal was allowed visitors. He was in an oxygen tent and had an i.v. tube in one arm. He was pale and thin and old. Out of his element, he could not project life. He did not look like he would live. Unfocused and tired, he could barely whisper. We left after a few minutes.

Alan, Mac, and I were still playing melodrama and Marlene was still coming with us. She was clamping an ever-stronger hold on me. She was feeding me, bedding me, and now I could not go anywhere without her. Wherever we went, she had me drive. I hated her luxury car. I hated its plush seats and indolent luxury. Most of all, I hated it because it was a symbol of my indenture. I did not have enough money to rent my own place and did not think of getting a job.

Meanwhile, Hal was growing stronger. I saw him every day, and if I did not go with Marlene, I would walk the two miles to the hospital. In a week, the oxygen tent was removed; instead, Hal had a tube in his nose. When I was alone with him Hal would say, "Kiddo, give me a cigarette."

I would say, "Hal, you're not supposed to smoke."

He would say, "Kiddo, if I can't smoke or drink or have any pleasures at all, what's the sense of living? I don't care what the doctor says."

"You sure, Hal?"

"Have you turned Baptist, son? Sounds like you've got religion. You're talking awful funny and you even look peculiar."

"No, I haven't turned Baptist."

"Presbyterian, then. They're awful straight laced."

"Yeah, Presbyterian. I ran into a church meeting by mistake the other night and got reformed."

"You don't say."

"Yeah."

"Do I have to ask you again?"

I would give in and hand Hal a cigarette and he would smoke with the oxygen running.

For two weeks Hal stayed in the hospital. During that time, Marlene bought two of Hal's paintings from Jerry. One was quite nice. It showed a farmhouse and horse at dawn with a yellow sky. She said, "I bought them just to help him out. They're not very good."

"I like them."

"Choose the one you'd like."

"No. Thanks, Marlene, I can't."

"Go ahead. They weren't expensive."

"No."

Every few days she repeated this. Finally I told her I would accept one, which made her happy. But knowing why she wanted me to have it, I never took it.

***

None of us—Mac, Alan, and me—had ever been to a Fiesta. Fiesta then was a three-day explosion of mariachi music, dancing, and open house parties across Santa Fe. It began on the Friday before Labor Day. The three of us were excited. We told Tiffany's two owners we would not perform a Friday night Fiesta show.

"You have an obligation to be here," they told us.

"No, we don't," Mac said.

I kept silent while the others argued. Within a few minutes they fired us.

The next Friday night was the opening of Fiesta. Mac and Alan, Marlene and I walked up Bishop's Lodge Road to Fort Marcy hill to the burning of Zozobra—Old Man Gloom—a huge fifty-foot puppet whose arms and head swiveled on cables. Zozobra (Gloom) was the creation of Hal's friend, Will Shuster. When Zozobra burned, one's troubles were erased. While this bug-eyed monster in white shirt and trousers stood still and silent on the top of Fort Marcy hill, hundreds stood by waiting for the fire dance of Jacques Cartier.

While we had walked up the hill, I became increasingly aware of the sickness of being with Marlene. Now, as we waited, she hooked an arm around one of mine. I froze. I was embarrassed to be seen with her. I scanned the crowd, hoping no one I knew was there. Almost at once I saw my college president and quickly turned my back.

Mac had disappeared but Alan was standing with us. Suddenly one of Zozobra's arms moved. That was my excuse to disentangle my arm and point, saying, "Look! It's moving!"

"Oh, yeah," Alan said.

We thought the festivities were beginning, but Mac returned, saying he had been moving the arms. Dark descended. A band assembled and played a march. Robed and hooded figures with torches marched at the foot of Zozobra. Candles and green flares lit the sky. At last Cartier came out, a Santa Fe legend, old and fragile, making tentative awkward steps. I expected him to tumble over. He danced towards the figure and away, forwards and backwards but always moving slightly closer, tantalizing the crowd that had come to see Zozobra wrapped in flames. Finally Cartier leaped forward and torched the old man's trousers. Zozobra looked down, saw the fire and roared, lifted one leg, then another. The flames grew bigger as they raced up his trousers. He waved his arms, turned his head, his mouth opening and shutting while big roars piped from invisible speakers.

Afterwards, as we drank in a downtown bar, Mac, Alan and Marlene laughed and shouted, but I thought, "I gotta get away," but after three drinks that feeling disappeared.

The next day Marlene went shopping. She always wanted me to go everywhere with her and I usually did, and hated myself for it. On this day I said I would not, that I was going later. When she left I packed my clothes in a bag and walked to the plaza where Mac was taking pictures of tourists.

Machad bought a camera and refitted it inside a box that he built, big enough to include a tray of developing fluid. He would develop sepia-toned photographs inside the box and mount the photographs on thick cardboard with a gold filigree border that he had printed. The photos looked like ones from the 1890s.

The plaza was mobbed and Mac was doing a good business. He was posing men in a sombrero and a pair of chaps borrowed from the melodrama.

I told Mac I was leaving Marlene and wanted to stow my bag in his car. I found the car a few blocks away and put my bag in the back of his unlocked trunk.

That night Marlene and I went with Mac and Alan to a downtown bar. The room was jammed: the tables were filled and people stood everywhere, talking loudly.

We had just stepped inside when above the noise I heard a shout, a wild southwestern voice booming across the room. I turned and saw Gene West standing at the bar. I turned to the others and said, "That's Gene West!" and pushed through the crowd towards him with the others right behind. I got in back of Gene and shouted hello. He turned, saw me and boomed "Bob!" We all shook hands.

Dressed in black western pants, a black knit sweater and black Stetson, his face creased and handsome, Gene looked like a movie star.

I yelled, "Tom Heath's having a party!" I had never met Heath, neither had Mac or Alan, but we had all heard of the party. In those days fiesta parties were open to all.

"Is he?" Gene said.

"Yeah! We gotta bring booze."

"Okay," he said, "let's make a run."

"I'll go with you," I said, wanting to get to know him, but Mac, who was more aggressive and used his deeper voice and hefty muscled frame, stepped forward and said, "No, I'm going. You stay here." Gene said the rest of us should stay there while he and Mac went for a bottle. When they returned I jumped in his car with Mac, leaving Alan with Marlene to follow us.

Tom Heath's house was jammed with characters from across New Mexico, as we discovered edging our way through rooms. Gene knew a few people, I knew none. I could not believe some of the people I saw—women done up in wild colored dresses and young bearded men in high boots and coats with gold trim and ribbons that made them look like pirates. What was this? Why were they in costumes? I had not yet heard of hippies.

Gene, if he noticed them, said nothing. I spent my time with him in Heath's kitchen. Gene was hungry and went to the refrigerator and pulled out a plate of beef bones with meat still on them. We got knives and whittled at the meat. As we were gnawing on the bones, Tom Heath walked in. I gathered it was Heath by the way he moved with authority, and by the fact that Gene, when he saw him, stood up briefly, shook hands and then ashamed (I thought) at having been caught stealing from the refrigerator, slunk back in his chair, head hanging down, nodding whenever Tom spoke.

When Tom left, Gene and I went onto Tom's back porch and sat on chairs. "Gene," I said, "I'd like to work for you." I liked Gene and wanted to work on a ranch, but more important I wanted to get rid of Marlene who was, right now, probably sloshing up a lot of booze in another room and making a fool of herself with her raucous Texas laugh.

"Bob," Gene said, "I don't have enough money to pay you. I have just enough to feed the family."

We had gone through this before at Hal's, and his answer had been the same. This time I had to press it. I leaned forward, almost pleading. "I'll work for nothing, Gene. I don't need the money. It doesn't matter."

He looked down, folded his hands, and stared at them awhile before he said, "Bob, I don't want to take advantage of you."

"Gene, you won't be." I waited till he looked up. "I've got to get away from Marlene. I've been staying at her house. She's hanging onto me. I've got to get away from her."

He groaned, turned his head sideways and shaking it, said, "I thought so." His mouth tightened. "That goddamned woman," he said, looking down. "Taking advantage of a young man. I hate those kind." He said it almost talking to himself, then looking up at me said, "Yes, Bob, you can come out."

I almost shouted. I could breathe again. "Thanks, Gene. Thank you." Now my problem was to tell Marlene. I was afraid she would whine or cry and I would break my resolve.

I went around the house collecting the others. We met at Marlene's and sat drinking until dawn. It was then I told her quietly and in front of the others that I was going to Gene's.

"Oh," she said, giving a little gasp, "all right."

That was all the emotion she showed. Gene stood up, thanked her, and he and I walked outside. The sky was now a lemon yellow in the east, the air cool. My eyes hurt from the smoke and alcohol. I was tired. I could have slept standing up.

Gene turned to me and asked, "Where are your things? You must have some stuff here."

"I put it in Mac's car. It's downtown."

Standing alongside his long red Buick Gene stuck his hands in his pockets, pulled out keys and handed them to me. "You drive, Bob." As I closed the door, Gene slumped in the seat beside me, pulling his hat over his face. I figured he always wanted to play the part of a big Texas rancher, and now he was beginning. After all, I was the hired man, so to speak, wasn't I?

FIVE

Chaquaco (summer 1966)

I cruised down the empty streets, heading us beyond Santa Fe to the Cerrillos flats. I did not really know Gene, who was now slumped beside me, his hat over his head. I did not know his family. But that was all right. I needed something new.

We rolled to the end of Canyon Road and headed for Mac's battered Mercedes which now sat alone on the street. Ten hours earlier the street had been jammed with cars. I pulled alongside the Mercedes. I had my hand on the door handle when Gene said, "You can't tell me you're not rich. Your father has money." This was the first thing he had said since we had gotten in the car.

Gene was looking at me, his hat now pushed back on his head.

"Yes," I said, "that's right. How did you know?"

"I can always spot 'em."

I lifted Mac's unlocked trunk and pulled out my two bags and laid them on Gene's back seat. But before I could drive off Gene started a conversation so intense I had to give it my full attention. We sat in his car discussing my life, discussing Marlene and my family, actually arguing. This continued as Gene directed me through narrow roads to a side street where he told me to park in front of a small adobe. Gene angled his long frame out of the car and ducked his head to keep from knocking his hat off. He hobbled around a street corner and opened a pale blue gate on the low adobe wall that surrounded the house. He jiggled the hook and finally shoved the gate open and hobbled to the front door. The entrance was two feet below ground. Gene began kicking the screen door and banging his fists on it and yelling, "Leon! Leon!"

I thought he wanted to thrash Leon, whoever he was. Gene had not mentioned him. No doubt Leon was someone he had encountered last night, someone who had insulted him or owed him money. Leon never came to the door.

Soon we were cruising through town again and onto the Albuquerque highway. I pushed the accelerator down and the Buick leaped to 75 mph. I headed the Buick through rangeland towards Cerrillos, past the penitentiary and clumps of sage that stood out clear against the red, cracked earth. I turned off the highway onto a rutted dirt road. "Slow down!" Gene hollered. "You'll break open the oil pan!" I remembered this road as we cut past a gorge, climbed a hill and passed a white frame house below, then ran past a homesteader's dugout. Finally the road climbed a rise with a windmill on top. Down below sat a house and corral. The house was surrounded by a coyote fence with a gate next to the corral. This was Chaquaco.

Gene opened the gate. As I drove through a dog ran at the car. I got out as the dog barked at me. Gene yelled, "Coyote! Shut up!"

I looked sideways at Coyote as I pulled my bags from the back seat. Gene said, "Pay him no mind, Bob."

I followed Gene inside, through a mudroom to the kitchen with a small unpainted table and chairs. The kitchen and living room were one space. The floors were cement. Gene led me through the kitchen to a bedroom.

"Sleep there, Bob," he said. "Get yourself some rest."

I put my bags down and stripped off my clothes. I crawled between the soothing sheets. The soft bed felt good. Aching with fatigue, I could hear Gene stumbling around and undressing in the room behind. I heard his bed creak as he got in and that was the last I heard.

Minutes later, it seemed, I heard someone stomping into the house. I heard the sound of boots on the floor, the door slamming and another door opening. I tried to open my eyes. The light hurt. Someone shouted, "Get up, you crazy sonofabitch!"

In the room behind I heard Gene say weakly, "Go away, Leon. Sit in the kitchen."

But Leon kept stomping towards my room. I opened my eyes and saw a short, lean man in worn jeans and western plaid shirt in the doorway. He saw me and pulled back his head, then walked through to Gene's room, bawling in a lilting Texas twang, "You're getting' up, you crazy bastard. Come hollering and screaming at five in the morning to get me up. Goddammit I'm up, now you're gettin' up."

Gene, his voice a bit stronger now, said, "Get in the kitchen, Leon. Make some coffee."

Leon started banging pots and pouring water. Soon I heard stirrings in the bedroom behind—Gene was dressing. He passed through my room with his pants undone and belt hanging out, shirt drooped over pants, bootless and hobbling. "Goddammit, Leon. Why'd you have to come now?"

"We're gong to get this show on the road, ain't we? I already passed by Archie's and got him up."

Gene groaned.

Leon said, "Well, hell, you started this. You came by my place at five."

By then I was sitting on the edge of my bed, dragging on my pants. I ambled fuzzy headed into the kitchen, which smelled of fresh coffee perking on the stove. Leon and I exchanged glances and askance hellos while Gene rumbled on. "You don't have to come with us, Bob. You go back to bed."

Something was happening, I did not know what, but whatever it was, I did not want to be left out. "Where you going?" I asked.

"Texas. Leon's going to buy some cows."

That settled it. This was the West—cattle country—and I had

never seen a cattle sale.

We drank coffee and smoked cigarettes, then piled into Leon's car and drove to the end of Gene's road to Hal's old place, where Archie now lived. Archie's was a nestle of well-plastered, small adobe buildings with a bare dirt yard, clean and raked and surrounded by a coyote fence and tall cottonwoods. Gene's house was surrounded with mesquite and tumbleweed that rolled almost to the front door.

It was now seven in the morning.

When Archie came out I saw he was a younger version of his dad, a handsome man with well-trimmed handle bar mustache, lean and neatly dressed in jeans and clean shirt. Gene decided that Archie would drive and I would relieve him. Meanwhile, I sat in the back with Leon, who pulled on a pint of Jim Beam.

We headed south to Clines Corners and then east on Route 66 towards Amarillo. Hours rolled on and we flew across New Mexico through Santa Rosa and Tucumcari to the Panhandle. Leon was supposed to meet Chuck Spradley in a café outside Nara Visa, New Mexico at one o'clock and from there we were going to Chuck's ranch. The three of them talked about the land we were crossing, compared it to their own and agreed it was not as good as theirs. They even got out once to examine the grass.

Gene and Leon talked about the old days of ranching in the Panhandle, who owned what ranch and when. At two in the afternoon we rolled up to the café. Chuck was not there. We sat at a booth and asked the waitress if he had been there. She said he had not. Had he left a message? No.

"That sonofabitch has forgot," Leon said, and after we had our coffee we drove into Texas, driving miles off the highway on a hard dirt road to Chuck's headquarters. He was not there, either. We sprawled on the grass behind his back porch.

We waited three hours, occasionally talking and napping. Each of us had had a hard night. Gene had been with Leon and Archie before I met him. They had been at the Plaza Bar when Archie and later Leon gave Gene the slip, so Gene said.

"I did not!" Leon laughed. "I was standin' right there at the bar. I turned around and you were gone."

We were hungry and decided to eat some of Chuck's food. He had left his back door open. His kitchen was white and bare and ghostly. There was nothing in the refrigerator except beer. We took it and Leon left him a note. Then, after lolling awhile longer on the grass in the chill dusk, we headed west into the oncoming New Mexico night.

Hours later we suffered the cap to this folly—a flat—as we drove a back- country dirt road near Cerrillos. I had not driven at all. Archie had driven both ways, and now he was fixing the flat. Archie left himself off at his home, and we returned to Gene's. Gene shook his head at Leon for this mad thirteen-hour, cross-country lunge on the slim chance we were going to meet Chuck Spradley.

***

After Leon left the next day, Gene and I took his pickup to a pasture to check on cattle. On the day after, Monday, Gene started me on my first job. He wanted the corral enlarged to include a holding pen that would allow cattle into the corral one at a time. He marked out the fence lines and measured off a spot every five feet for postholes. Nearby lay a pile of railroad ties. Gene gave me a post-hole digger, a shovel and a tamp and left for a construction job.

I dug the holes three feet deep and slipped in the eight-foot ties. A post-hole digger has two handles, with a shovel at each end. In three hours I had about eight posts sunk and had begun nailing boards to them, on three levels. As I hammered, I heard a distant thundering. The sound grew louder. Curious, I stopped work and straightened. Whatever was making the noise was coming towards me from beyond the nearby rise. I recognized hoof beats. Suddenly horses' heads appeared over the top of the rise. Then necks, shoulders, and legs appeared. The horses were now galloping down the hill towards me. They are after water, I thought. Terrified, I clambered up the fence I had just built and sat atop a post, lifting my feet as high as I could. The horses came on a gallop towards me. I prayed they would not come near me. God alone knew what they would do, maybe snap at my heels, crowd around the post rearing up, trying to strike me, biting my legs, those big teeth tearing out hunks of flesh.

To my surprise they seemed not to notice me. They slowed to a trot when they approached the corral. They walked to the trough that lay only feet from me. They drank. They would lift their heads, look about, and dip them again in water. After they had drunk their fill, they trotted off. When they were fifty yards away, I climbed down.

That night Gene inspected my work and liked it. The next day, after Gene drove off, I continued the work. In a few days the holding pen was finished, except for the gate. With the scraps of lumber that were left, Gene arranged the boards to show me what he wanted. Again he left. I took tools from the shed alongside the stables, measured my pieces, then cut. By mid-morning the gate was finished, only waiting for Gene to hang it. My first ranch job was complete.

***

In the evenings Gene and I talked as we sat around the small brown kitchen table. From the table you could see out the windows on three sides of the house—to the windmill in back, the stables and work shed to the side, and the corral in front.

Looking to the horizon I would think of Wyoming and Montana to the north, and of all the plains and cut gorge earth stretching from Mexico clear to Canada. It seemed a land without time. It seemed all the more so because there were no electric lights at Chaquaco—the West's home. We lit the house at night with kerosene lamps and when we wanted to take a bath we heated water on the gas stove.

Gene and I talked late into the evenings. At dusk we would lift the globes from the kerosene lamps and trim the wicks. We would light the wicks and replace the globe and adjust the knob for a higher or lower flame. As the dark grew outside, so the yellow circle of light grew around the lamps on the brown table and our glasses of amber whiskey. That first night Gene told me that Genie and Margaret were in Utah with his eldest daughter, Diane, and would be back in two weeks. Susie, his youngest daughter, lived in the one-story white frame house a few miles down the road.

"Her husband," Gene explained, "is in Vietnam."

I had seen Tom at the July branding. At that time he had probably received his draft notice.

Once Gene's construction job in town ended and he spent his days on the ranch, he would take me with him on errands to buy hay, or to see Susie, or to drive the pastures to inspect his small herd of 150 head. Then he would buy us lunch at Horseman's Haven, a diner where other small ranchers came to chat.

About two weeks after I came to Chaquaco, Gene and I had chores in town. We finished them and went to Hal's.

"Gene," Hal said, "how's old Bob working out?"

"He's doin' a fine job, Harold. He built me a holding pen." Gene looked at me with approval.

"Don't say." Hal turned to me. "I'm glad to hear it, son, and I'm proud of you." He smiled mischievously.

"How're you feeling, Harold?"

"I'm a little weak, Gene, but I'm not complaining. This problem is keeping me out of circulation, but I manage okay."

"Is there anything we can get you?"

"No. Friends see to most of my needs. Marlene's been good to me. She comes by every day, does my shopping for me."

I wondered what Marlene was thinking, if she was lonely, if she was hurt. But I did not care.

We got up to go.

"Well," Hal said, "it's good to see both of you."

"Good to see you, Hal," I said. "Glad you're better."

"You just do what Gene tells you and you'll do well."

Gene and I drove downtown to La Fonda for a drink. Afterwards we walked under the portale next to the plaza. A car of teenagers in t-shirts drove slowly by, blasting music and shouting.

Gene said, "The goddamn boys today aren't worth a damn. They just don't have any goddamn decency, can't do the right thing." He put a hand over his eyes, staggered, and sobbed. He stopped, took his hand from his face and walked to a post on the portale. He leaned against it and sobbed again. "Bob, what the hell ever happened to honor? What happened to this generation?"

"I don't know."

"The goddamn bastards tell a girl they love her, get her to believe it, get her pregnant and leave her. They don't have any goddamn guts!" He broke out crying, his chest jerking as he heaved out hard sobs.

"Margaret's had a baby up in Utah. The goddamn son of a bitch just dropped her flat."

I had never seen a man cry in public. I had never even seen a man cry. When Gene straightened I crooked an arm in his and we walked slowly off.

***

My next job was to build a wall to enclose a flower garden for Genie.

"Genie's wanted a flower garden for years," Gene said, "but I just haven't been able to get around to it."

Gene explained what he wanted. I was to dig a trench two-feet deep and one-foot wide in the shape of an L, connecting a corner of the living room with a corner of the porch. When that was done I was to build a form from planks—a wall on both sides of the trench—rising a foot or so above ground. Then I was to fill the form with a mixture of cement and rock.

Gene came home after my second day's work and saw the forms were not right. The top plank for one section stuck out too far and I had already poured the cement into the form. The process was to drive stakes on either side of the trench and hold the planks to the stakes with baling wire. I had had trouble with the baling wire. When he saw the mess I had made of it, Gene was angry, but only briefly. "Well, Bob," he said, "it'll be a real Santa Fe wall," meaning the walls would not be regular, but wavy.

When the foundation was completed I built the wall with adobe bricks Gene had laid nearby. I mixed mud and straw for mortar. The mixture's consistency had to be thick. I shoveled my dirt into a wheelbarrow, added straw and water and mixed with a hoe. As the mixture thickened I would raise the hoe up high and slam it into the mixture and pull it towards me.

If there was too much dirt, I added water. If I had too much water, I added dirt. Again and again I lifted the hoe, slammed it down, and pulled it towards me. When the mud, water and straw were thoroughly mixed I scooped mortar with a shovel and laid it on the cement. I troweled it out and laid adobes on it. I was learning Southwest culture firsthand. .

On my next lesson, horseback riding, I overcame my fear of horses. Gene rode a beautiful, spirited palomino; I rode a chestnut quarter horse. I watched Gene saddle and bridle the horses, but the first time I bridled the chestnut, Gene came to the stable, looked at the bridle and removed it. "That," he said, "would have been the ride of the century."

***

It was not clear to me just how tough things were for the Wests. I did not realize how little money anybody made raising beef. Perhaps I thought Gene made good money at construction. Genie worked in town as a seamstress at a fashionable boutique and Margaret was a teller at the Bank of Santa Fe.

When Margaret and Genie returned several weeks after fiesta, they brought Margaret's baby boy with them. Margaret and her son moved in with Susie.

Genie was a short, rosy-cheeked woman with a great smile. But at that time she was not smiling. On the day of her return, she and Gene and I sat in the kitchen and Gene told her that I would be working there until fall semester started in October. Gene mentioned that he was going to pay me a little something before I returned to school. Genie said, "You didn't promise to pay him? Where are you going to get the money?"

"That's all right," I said. "I don't need to be paid."

"He shouldn't have promised you, Bob."

"I'll pay him something," Gene muttered.

Genie gave him a look; her eyes flashed and her mouth was set. Gene said nothing more.

SIX
St. John's (1966-67)

During my first year at St. John's, the country was becoming increasingly engaged in a war in Vietnam, but it was not something Mac and I, or Alan, talked about. We did not read newspapers; we did not watch television. The war was not a part of our lives, but it was ever-present, like a distant drumbeat.

While I was at Chaquaco, Mac spent his days memorizing Greek vocabulary. But before he could take his Greek exam and be admitted to his sophomore year, Mac's draft board ordered him to report for his physical examination in Albuquerque. Soon after, while I was still living at Chaquaco, Mac left for boot camp.

Since it focused on Greek language, philosophy and literature, freshman studies had a beautiful unity. Sophomore year had no such unity. In seminar we studied Roman writers and philosophers, medieval Christian theologians and Renaissance humanists. As a cursory introduction to these writers, the seminar was a success. But what one gleaned from it was another matter. There were no themes pulling this disparity of texts together. Nor was any attempt made to discover the morphology of classical or western civilizations. Perhaps the tutors, with one exception, thought this disparate list of books to be beads on a single cultural string. For this and other problems I had with the program, this year at St. John's was as useless as my year at Columbia.

With Mac gone, a spirit of play departed from the college. And once Gail and the boys returned to Santa Fe, I saw little of Alan. My experience the previous summer, not to mention my previous life experiences, distanced me from other students.

Our dining club continued with new members, but we had few guests. Hal, Gene and Genie came one night, and Archie and Hal came another. The night Gene and Genie came, Gene wore a suit that hung on his gangly frame; he called it his "Cary Grant suit." But Gene's western manners and stance could never be mistaken for those of a polished urbanite. Gene was thoroughly western.

When the school year drew to a close, I returned to Chaquaco.

SEVEN
Chaquaco (Summer 1967)

Rodeo de Santa Fe is held each year on the third weekend in June. Each of Gene's three daughters—Margaret, Susie, and Diane—had been rodeo queens. This year's queen was Brenda Hapgood, who lived with her parents on the Las Vegas highway.

Being selected rodeo queen is an honor in ranching country. The queen is feted by community groups, gets her picture in the newspaper and rides at the head of the rodeo parade, surrounded by her court.

One of the biggest events of rodeo week is the rodeo dance. This year it was being held at La Fonda. Susie was anxiously looking forward to the dance, held the night before the opening of the rodeo. Since Tom was in the army, Susie wanted me to take her to the dance.

Her parents were all for it. Of course I did not have cowboy clothes. I did not have jeans, or western shirt, or hat, just old denims and khaki shirts I used to wear. There was a western hat I wore when working but I used to flatten the brim, which was otherwise curved up.

Hats were a big thing, and still are. The style then and now in New Mexico and Texas is to curve the brims sharply up. If you look at old photos of the 1920s you see the men wearing flat, wide-brimmed Tom Mix hats. Look at older western photos and you will see many styles of hats among one group of men. The present-day men of cattle country want to conform to one image, just as urban businessmen want to conform to another. Anyone who does not turn his brim all the way up, unless he is a buckaroo from Nevada or Utah, would probably be considered a dude.

I thought going to the rodeo dance would be a real dud. In the first place, I did not know any of the cowboys. For another those I had talked to I thought rather dim. I was particularly apprehensive when Susie made it clear that I was going to have to wear some new jeans, a flashy shirt, a hat and boots. I said I did not want to; Genie said I had to.

Susie said, "He'll fit into Tom's jeans."

"Bob," said Genie, "you'll fit into one of Gene's shirts."

"He'll have to have some boots, mommy."

"Well," said Genie, "see if he won't fit into a pair of Tom's."

Susie jumped up, ran to her pickup and drove off. Fifteen minutes later she was back with a pair of jeans and boots. "Go inside and try these on."

Genie left the room to get one of Gene's shirts.

Ten minutes later I was in my bedroom, trying on the clothes. When I came out, Susie squealed, "Oh, Bob, you look great."

It was the first time I had ever worn a pair of high-heeled boots and I was having a hard time with them. Normally I wore a pair of workman's boots, even when riding. I got out of the clothes quick and back into my normal duds.

Two nights later came the big event. I squeezed into Tom's jeans and boots, Gene's shirt and hat.

Susie was working downtown that day and was going to meet me at La Fonda. I arrived in town by dusk and hobbled across the plaza towards La Fonda. I was crossing San Francisco Street approaching several tourists when one of them said something like, "Take it easy, cowboy." I already felt uncomfortable in these boots and clothes, and now felt more so.

I met Susie in La Fonda's lobby, and we walked to the room rented for the occasion. A western band was playing, and the room was already filled with cowboys and cowgirls, none of whom I had ever seen before. Susie was dressed in a tight pair of blue jeans with a plaid shirt and a hat with the brims turned up. And wearing boots, of course.

Everyone, no doubt, had already had his share of bourbon, the preferred drink in ranching country. I bought us bourbon and water and we downed our drinks and got to dancing. That was one thing I loved, western dancing. We danced just about every tune, fast and slow, Texas two-stepping across the room, swinging to the beat, dipping, turning, swinging. It was great. My fears were wearing off. We were surrounded by a couple of hundred cowboys and their women, hundreds of men and women wearing hats and dancing. Men leaning over their women and propelling them backwards. Lead hands clasped together, the man's free hand grasped around the woman's waist, her free hand on his shoulder, her chin resting on his other shoulder or pressed against his chest. Heels scuffing against the floor, kicking up on the beat.

Susie and I were into it. My fears were wearing off. Then we got bumped. Rather Susie got bumped. I looked to see a big, beefy guy and his smirking woman glide off.

"Hey!" Susie said, "watch where you're going."

The guy said nothing, just kept gliding. Minutes later he was back to bump Susie again. This time she was offended, hurt, and knew it was intended as an insult. According to the western code my role required me to call the guy out, tell him to knock the shit off or I would remake his face. I could not figure out why he had picked us, but I was not going to get stomped by this guy. I was just an imitation cowboy. I was sorry for Susie but there was nothing I would do. She was trying to ignore it, but it happened again, twice more. We tried to keep away from them, and worked another part of the dance floor.

They did not bother us again. We danced and drank and had a good time. And when the dance was closing down, Lon Barrett, a neighbor of Gene's came around to say that he had gotten permission to open the sheriff posse's hall and we would all go there to continue the festivities. The hall was on the Albuquerque highway towards Chaquaco.

By the time we arrived I was well soaked with bourbon. The hall was small and crowded. We had all brought bottles. The band came too. After a few turns on the dance floor I was standing and taking a sip from my bottle when this short guy in a hat came up to me and said, "I hear you've been sayin' words about, Brenda Hapgood, the rodeo queen."

I had not said anything about Brenda Hapgood. I had never seen her except at a distance and I had certainly never talked about her, or to her. I could see that this guy wanted a fight. It did not dawn on me to run. I was drunk enough to be mean. He was not going to back me down or get any word out of me like, "Well you must be mistaken, I didn't say anything about Brenda Hapgood." He would have said, "Shut your fuckin' mouth, asshole. You say something about a woman, you better have the fuckin' guts to take the consequences."

I just looked at him, waiting for him to make the first move.

"Let's go to the men's room," he said and walked off.

I followed.

The men's room was small. As soon as I got in he had his fists up. I was nervous, maybe shaking slightly, but I put mine up too. Again I was waiting for him to make the first move. Then I got hit and the world went dark.

I was standing in the dancehall and Lon Barrett was next to me with his arm on my shoulder. Apparently he was speaking to me. "Are you okay?"

I could not think, my mind was foggy, my head hurt. I was wobbling and drunk, but otherwise okay. I looked at him. "Yeah."

"I didn't want to hurt you but we can't have fighting in this hall. I'm responsible. I gave my word to the sheriff's posse there wouldn't be any trouble."

Did what?

"I'm responsible for this hall. We can't have any fights."

I do not remember driving back to Chaquaco. The next day I lay around, hung over. That evening when Gene returned he told us, "I ran into Lon Barrett this afternoon. He apologizes for having to knock you out."

"Who were you fighting?" Margaret wanted to know.

"I don't know."

"He was fightin' Red Smith," Gene said. Gene turned to me. "Lon said you were whippin' the hell out of the judge."

"Judge?" I said.

"Rodeo judge."

"Red Smith!?" Margaret almost yelled. "I'd be ashamed of Bob if he couldn't whip that shrimp!"

"Lon couldn't allow any fighting at the sheriff's posse."

That apparently was why he knocked us out.

"He wants to make it up to you and says he'd like you to come out and work a day."

I never did take Lon up on his offer.

In those days the old culture of Santa Fe bar fighting was still strong. I witnessed and came close to witnessing several other bouts that summer. The second brawl, or stomping, came a week after the rodeo dance at a party in a hotel suite jammed with rodeo cowboys. I was there with Gene and Genie. This time I was dressed in khakis and wore shoes, not boots, and did not wear a hat. The only other person beside myself who was not a part of the culture was a middle-aged man who sat in the middle of the room with a pretty young woman. I was sitting by myself. Gene and Genie were across the room. A rodeo cowboy approached two others sitting in front of me and whispered, "We're going to get Mr. Slick. Pass the word." And one of them leaned over and whispered it to another.

I was sure that I was "Mr. Slick" since I was not wearing western clothes. Then I looked again at the middle-aged man who was still smiling and talking confidently to the young woman— the cowboys' "woman." She was smiling back at him. I realized he was Mr. Slick and was blithely unaware of what was planned for him.

I went to Gene and said, "Let's go. There's going to be trouble," and the three of us left, just before Mr. Slick was stomped by a roomful of rodeo cowboys.

My southwestern education continued later that summer when Gene and Genie and I, and perhaps Susie, went to the Mineshaft, a restaurant and bar in Madrid. Madrid was a ghost town twenty miles up the road from Cerrillos and had been a populous mining town but now the miner's shacks stood gray and weathered and deserted on the hillsides. The Mineshaft was now the only business in town. We went there to dance but instead of the ranching crowd, the room was packed with Hispanics. We danced and drank, but at some point one Hispanic man made the mistake of asking another man's girl to dance. I heard an argument behind me, and this time it was Gene who said, "Let's go."

A fight broke out and the Wests and I made a break for the parking lot. We were halfway across the stone and gravel lot when the fight spilled outside with men and women throwing rocks at one another. As we hustled away Gene said, "The Mexicans don't consider the evening a success unless they have a fight."

Fifty years later, when I talked with Sue (no longer "Susie") about some of her father's fights, she said, "Daddy loved to fight." But though he loved to fight, Gene knew when fighting was pointless.

***

That summer I spent many days by myself at Chaquaco, riding fence. I rode a gelding that was not named until after I left. He was a sweet, docile horse. He never gave a sign that I was cinching him too tight. Only by the end of the summer did I see that I had caused him sores, big clumps of flesh under the place of the cinch strap. Next year Gene wrote me in New York to say that they had sometimes called him "Bob" and sometimes "Wolf," and that he had eaten locoweed and had to be put down.

But that summer I saw as much of Bob as I did any person. We rode all day. I would leave in the morning with a bag filled with a strand of barbed wire, heavy gloves, and a cutting tool that was also a clamp. I would follow the fence line looking for breaks. When I found a break I would cut a short length of barbed wire from the strand. I would twist it onto to one end of the broken wire and pull the wire until I could twist the other end of the strand to the other end of the broken wire. I did this all day. I would saddle up early in the morning and ride until noon, return to the house for a sandwich and ride again. I might ride for six hours.

At this time Gene was picking up whatever work he could. One day he had a job in Santa Fe removing a dead horse from someone's property. He drove his skid loader and I followed in his pickup, moving slowly the twenty-five miles to Santa Fe to a house in the country. We secured one end of a heavy chain under the horse's front legs and over its back. The other end Gene secured to the skid loader's bucket. I pulled the pickup next to the horse. Gene raised the bucket and hoisted the dead horse. He turned the loader and the horse swung back and forth. He moved the loader forward and lowered the horse onto the bed of the pickup. Creeping down the highway we returned to Chaquaco where we reattached the chain—still around the horse—to the skid load-er's bucket and dumped the horse in an arroyo.

***

Most evenings Gene, Genie and I sat around the kitchen table or the living room, reading by the light of kerosene lamps. On Saturday nights we went dancing. Since there was no hot water tank at Chaquaco, we spent an hour or two heating water on the stove and took turns taking baths. Most times we went to a honkytonk on the outskirts of Santa Fe, but occasionally we drove the sixty miles to Albuquerque.

Life was simple, uncomplicated. Then Sean Fitzpatrick arrived in Santa Fe after two years in Vietnam. I had seen him several times before he shipped out, whenever he returned on leave. The Army was changing him.

As soon as he returned to the States he wrote me to say he was coming to Santa Fe. I asked Gene if he could visit Chaquaco and Gene said yes. During his brief time at Chaquaco, Sean went with me and the Wests and Leon to a dinner in the country. We all sat out of doors around a large table. Gene and Leon were drinking and arguing about the war. In those years everyone thought about the war. The war was omnipresent; arguments could spring up at any time. Leon had served in the Korean War; Gene had never served. I had heard them argue once before about the war. Leon always said we had no business there and Gene said we sure as hell did. As the argument this evening got hotter, Leon called Gene a chicken hawk and Gene knocked Leon out of his chair. Margaret began screaming; Genie yelled for Gene to stop. Years later Sue was to tell me that that was not the only time Gene had whipped his best friend.

There were three bedrooms in Gene's house, all laid out like cars on a train, one after another. Sean and I slept together in the last bedroom. Sean had been drinking this one night. Gene was a natural actor, and was often on stage in private life. Part of his persona was an affected whine, used sparingly, usually when he wanted to complain of someone or something. On this particular night we were in our room and Sean, who had been drinking, said in a loud voice, "The old man's a whiner." I knew that Gene in the next bedroom heard him. I said nothing to quiet Sean. The next morning Gene told me, "Tell you friend he has to leave this morning."

Sean found an apartment in Santa Fe and I saw little of him for the rest of the summer. He was drinking heavily, spending his days at the Plaza Bar from the time it opened until it closed. Finally he left for the east coast, and for over a year I did not see him.

Not long after Sean left, in mid-August, I had decided to leave the Wests. I was becoming uneasy with Gene: every time he asked me to do something, I heard an order. I had also decided to transfer back to Columbia where I would earn my degree in one year rather than in two, if I remained at St. John's.

Peter Schultz was throwing a party for everyone he knew in Santa Fe. Peter had said to bring the Wests, whom he knew from our dinner club. Peter's home was one of the last on Upper Canyon Road, in the Sangre de Cristo foothills. Gene, Genie, Margaret and I dressed up one Saturday afternoon and headed for Santa Fe in two cars. We stopped at Hal's to pick him up..

When we got there a crowd had already gathered. Among them were a few St. John's students along with some hippies and two tutors, Sam Brown and Fred and Lena Hooper. Peter was roasting a goat in a pit outside. Indoors his girlfriend laid out huge bowls of salads, punch and bread. I spent my time talking to students I had not seen in many months, and not enjoying myself.

Fred Hooper introduced Gene to Sam Brown, and while Gene was busy charming Sam I stepped outside.

When I returned, I made myself a drink and walked into the living room where Hal, Gene and Sam Brown were joking. Hal was wearing a pair of fake glasses with distorted eyes painted on them. Everyone was laughing, especially Gene. He had seen Harold's act with glasses a hundred times but always laughed. Then they were looking at me, still laughing.

Gene called out, "Come here, Bob." I walked closer and Gene called, "Get Harold a drink."

I stood a moment looking at the laughing crowd. I was sure Gene had said something like, "Watch this boy. I can make him do anything." My face tightened and I walked into the kitchen, thinking, "This will be the last time I ever do anything for you or your brother." I poured the drink and walked stiffly back through the crowd. They were still laughing. I gave the drink to Hal. He laughed some more.

Gene stood in the corner. I asked him, "Why did you call me over? Just to get a drink for Harold?"

"No, I wanted you to see Harold's face."

"Why didn't he get his own drink? Why didn't you get it? I'm leaving, Gene. I'm not your flunky."

Gene looked down at his drink and said nothing. He walked over to Genie and soon they were lugging their belongings to the car. Gene announced to the group we were leaving.

Sam walked from the other side of the room with a beaming face and called out to me, "Guess what? We'll be going to Gene's this Sunday!"

'Well, I won't be there. I'm leaving the ranch."

"Why? What happened?"

"I can't say any more now."

"Oh . . . I'd like to see you before you go."

"I'm transferring to Columbia next year."

"What? I thought you had more sense."

"I can finish there in one year. It's time I got down to work."

We shook hands and I went over to the Hoopers and I told them what I told Sam and said goodbye. They said that transferring to Columbia was better than staying at St. John's and wished me luck.

Everyone except Gene and I left in Margaret's car. Gene drove slowly down Canyon Road to Hal's as we talked, sometimes stopping. It was raining. The sky was dismal.

Gene told me, "I'm very sorry you feel that way, Bob. I never meant to use you like a flunky. There were a lot of jobs at the ranch that needed doing, that's true. But they've gone undone for years. I had you out there because I liked having you around. I enjoyed your company."

I said very little for the rest of the trip.

EIGHT
NEW YORK (1967-68)

Each week, it seems in retrospect, I watched another freak plod down one sidewalk or another. One man in a shapeless black overcoat trudged slowly, his feet enveloped in enormous coverings taped with black plastic. Another had no feet but long thin flippers. No heels or toes, but long pointy black flippers. And the prostitutes . . . The ugliest of the district's prostitutes, whom I saw every day walking 96th Street, was somewhere in her sixties. Perhaps she just seemed that old because her body was decayed. She was in the last stage of syphilis. Large bumps covered her long, boney face.

Years later the buildings on 96th Street were renovated and gentrified. But in the late sixties, not only were the buildings shabby, the streets were littered with newspapers and other debris.

I was living in upper West Side Manhattan, on the edge of the Needle District, a neighborhood inhabited by grotesques. These were not simply the impoverished and decrepit—they were that— but they comprised a freak show marching up and down 96th and adjacent streets.

One dusk I walked down 96th to my apartment and saw a small cluster of people gathered on the sidewalk next to the curb. As I approached I saw a body laying in the gutter, face up. I felt nothing, not even disgust. I was used to the filth of upper West Side Manhattan. I struck up a conversation with a man standing next to me. We joked about the man lying at our feet, dead from an overdose. We talked as we waited for police to arrive.

The man said the dead man made him think of a dying man in a phone booth making his last call. His call is interrupted by a recording saying, "Please deposit another twenty-five cents." The man does not have the money. The recording says, "I'm sorry, but your time is up." The man falls dead.

We laughed. What did this body matter? What did one more

dead man matter? The city was a shambles. The country was a shambles. America was on fire. New York was a mass of people and therefore a mass of contradictions.

The easy answer to surviving the chaos, perhaps the sensible one, was to grab the life raft nearest at hand. Each of the many rafts had a label: "Anti-War," "Dropout," "Law and Order," "Civil Rights," "Drugs," "Rich—Don't Bother Me." Everyone, except me and the walking dead on 96th, seemed to have pulled himself up on one raft or another.

My roommate, Edward, had most likely found his raft several years earlier. He had no self-doubts. He was applying to the State Department. with cities in flames and men and women burning alive in Vietnam, Raymond navigated his course far above the chaos swimming around him. He and his girlfriend went to posh restaurants most nights. I seldom saw them, except mornings. In the midst of America's moral confusion with about and below him, yet he maintained a steady course towards   the State Department.

I had returned to Manhattan in late summer and registered as an undergraduate philosophy major. Edward, a high school friend from New Canaan, had just graduated from Columbia College and was enrolled in the School of International Studies. We collided on the Columbia campus, went for a beer and decided to room together. Edward found us an apartment on 96the Street, on the edge of the Needle District.

The apartment was on the third floor of a walk up. The steps were old marble worn smooth. The walls of the lobby and stairway were dull and shabby. The apartment was small. It had two bedrooms, a kitchen, a living room and bath.

Narrow airshafts separated our building from two adjoining buildings. My bedroom window faced one airshaft, my roommate's another. In warm weather when everyone kept their windows open, we heard talk and shouting from both buildings. Whenever our neighbors finished a bottle of liquor, they dropped it down an airshaft. Every day we heard bottles smashing. A man with a safety helmet swept up the broken glass once or twice a week. Once someone tried to hit him with a bottle.

Our apartment was half a block from Riverside Drive with its swank apartments and three-story townhouses. Facing the drive was Riverside Park, and below that the Hudson River. Broadway was two blocks the other direction, and a world away. Every day as I walked up 96th Street to Broadway or from Broadway back to the apartment, I encountered the realm of the dead.

***

Edward's aggression and self-absorption gave him an enviable certitude and confidence. The chaos floated, swarmed, and roiled about and below him, yet he maintained a steady course towards the State Department.

We came from the same background. As children we had been neighbors and played together. We both read Sir Walter Scott's medieval romances; we bought lead footman and knights, built papier-mâché castles and waged battles. We even dressed as knights and went in search of adventures in the woods. My younger sister, who had a crush on Edward, was our page.

That stage of the mind's development—the romantic stage—is essential to an artist of any kind. It remained a guiding force in my life, leading me to adventure across the country to seek out people and land and customs of a kind I had never encountered before. The romantic urge died early in Edward. Having left New Canaan High School for an elite prep school may have had an influence. But by age twenty-one, the boy who had written a medieval saga of his own, "The Last Templar," and who once wanted to be a writer, was now a hardened realist who would eventually make himself a place on President Reagan's National Security Council alongside Oliver North and John Poindexter. By that time an expert on South American affairs, Edward had suggestions on the Iran Contra, guns-for-hostages deal.

While Edward played by the rules (and played them) and forged on, taking advantage of every opportunity and of every person who could further his ambition, I floundered. Where was certitude? There was none. History had no course or line of movement, no direction. Brute force was the law of politics, national and international. Brute force governed all affairs, subtly and not so subtly.

***

The degradation I saw daily on the streets made my study of philosophy all the more irrelevant. I was a philosophy major. I wanted the rigor of a discipline that could clarify ideas. The professors at Columbia's philosophy department were analytic philosophers. At its best analytic philosophy is a form of grammatical and logical analysis. The analytic philosophy texts I studied at Columbia in 1963 were wonderfully clear and incisive. Naturally I thought that more analytic philosophy would be equally useful.

I registered for a course in the theory of knowledge and another in the philosophy of science. Had I suddenly arrived on Earth from the dark side of the moon, I could not have been more lost. Our texts were massive, obscure tomes written by Columbia professors. Neither had anything relevant to say about a world in chaos. Still, I tried to struggle through them, but their irrelevance combined with my thick-headedness unsettled me as much as the walking dead on 96th Street.

At root analytic philosophy is antithetic to meaning itself. The analytic philosopher might retort that meaning was a private matter, independent of the discipline. But the young, unformed mind soon learns that meaning, or what meaning he might attach to anything, including his own life, is arbitrary. Even opposition to the Vietnam War was arbitrary. One cannot connect logical and grammatical analysis to value. In fact, value judgments were a particular target of analytic philosophy.

Plato, Socrates, Lao Tzu, Confucius and hundreds of other philosophers and sages who had shored up civilization for thousands of years were now informed that they were, at best, irrelevant.

***

The world degenerated into a kaleidoscope of events without order. To the waking mind, the rational mind, time and events proceeded in jerky, stop-frame images. The subterranean mind was trying to make sense of the chaos in the big world. It could not.

Nor could the waking mind. Some part of me was unresponsive, aware but blocking the meanings behind the images. The outer shell kept moving, going about its business, but the subterranean mind, not making sense of anything, absorbed and felt everything.

To this day events of that year remain a chaos of images.

I had no television but read an occasional newspaper, feeding my mind with images of smashed store windows, glass in the streets, fires, photos of bagged bodies.

An older cousin, who was something of a smart alec, asked me how I felt about the war. "I haven't made up my mind," I told him. "I haven't enough information." He said, smiling, "I've got it here in my jacket pocket," and reached inside his sports coat.

One afternoon in early April I returned to New York on the New Haven Railroad. As I had done many times in the past, I got off at the 125th Street station and in late afternoon walked across Harlem to Morningside Heights and up the steep bank to campus. Several hours later Martin Luther King, Jr. was murdered.

Riots erupted in Cleveland, Baltimore, Washington, D.C., Chicago, and Louisville. Edward said, "If I was black I'd be the worst one on the streets!" Edward knew what the score was. But did Edward care?

Columbia students seized Hamilton Hall. Then word had it that Harlem blacks had seized it. Had they? I was not sure what was happening. Then I heard that Harry Coleman, a New Canaan neighbor and dean of Columbia College, had been shot in the chest in his office by a deranged student.

For days we were kept off campus, which was surrounded by a ring of blue-uniformed police. When classes resumed, I saw a younger acquaintance from New Canaan sitting on a window ledge of Low Library. That too had been seized. I called out, "What's a nice boy like you doing up there?" He waved and smiled. I was apolitical and could not understand why someone would want to be a part of the occupation. I could understand black anger but not the action of middle-class white kids. To me the occupation was a stunt.

For the last two years, living a life of irresponsibility at an ivory tower school outside a lovely city, working on a ranch and playing melodrama in summers, I was blissfully unaware of police brutality and misconduct. I was surprised, then, when a cop on the Columbia cordon came up to me and whispered, "Fuck you" in my ear. I looked at him, totally uncomprehending. Later I understood that he wanted me to yell at him so he could club me.

In those days of anger black men and women panhandled from whites. Perhaps one might feel white guilt or fear and hand one a quarter. I decided to turn tables. I dressed in a tweed sports jacket, put on a tie and headed for Broadway. I approached blacks and asked, "Can you help me out with a little money?"

Surprisingly I do not remember anyone denying me. I stood outside a bar and saw a prosperous looking black woman walking towards me. I asked her for money. She looked in her purse and told me, "Wait here," went inside the bar to get change and came back with a dollar.

A girlfriend and I went with my friend Larry Blake and his girlfriend to watch an anti-war demonstration at Grand Central Station. We stood on the main floor not far from the demonstrators, who were chanting and holding signs. We stood near the stairs leading to the Vanderbilt Avenue exit. We were lucky to be standing near there. A mass of blue-uniformed police came through the 42nd Street doors, formed into a phalanx and charged the demonstrators, billy clubs in hands. The four of us turned and ran up the stairs, turned at the loge and watched. The police were clubbing everyone in sight, even commuters with briefcases, the stolid Republicans who thought the war a fine and lovely thing. We paused only a moment, then fled outside onto Vanderbilt Avenue.

In these years the certitude Father had lived by began crumbling. He had lived his work life among the senior management of international firms and now announced, "Doing business is little more than putting a gun to somebody's head." Amidst the madness of 1968 I told him I felt that Mass Man might revolt against the ruling class and attack the rich. "You may be right," he said.

***

Chaos was universal. Whatever common assumptions held post-World War II American society together—a society in which the

G.I. Bill sent many thousands of men to colleges and created unprecedented prosperity for millions of Americans—that society was now fractured, fearful and angry.

What had education, if anything, to do with this? America had been founded by an educated patrician class whose minds were formed by the liberal arts and by common notions, including the role of law in civil society. But by the time of the founders the underpinnings of a unified culture had already cracked as a consequence of rapid and ongoing scientific discoveries and their practical applications. The traditional liberal arts curriculum of the Middle Ages, which consisted of mathematics and language arts, eventually split into the sciences and the humanities. Well before the time I arrived at Columbia, the humanities had lost their coherence in a multitude of specialties.

My years at Columbia were an intellectual grab bag. a crazy quilt of unrelated courses. I learned a few skills, yes, but nothing to help me or my contemporaries make sense of our country or the world. The students who raged against the Establishment were equally confused, for American college and university education did not present a coherent picture of the world. There was none. But what else could one expect from a culture lacking common notions?

The education by which a culture hopes to mold its people is, after all, a reflection of that culture. When a culture such as ours is chaos of conflicting ideologies, it has no shared idea of what virtues best preserve it, and is incapable of designing an education intended to develop the individual with the civic and intellectual virtues needed to maintain it. Lacking these, dangerous energies are released.

When Dwight Eisenhower was president of Columbia University he challenged a faculty member to explain the virtues of a value-free education. "What good," he asked, "are exceptional physicists, unless they are exceptional Americans?" The faculty thought this naïve.

A year or more before the Columbia student take-over, former University of Chicago chancellor Robert Hutchins agreed with Eisenhower. In an essay, "Permanence and Change,"

Hutchins wrote that liberal arts colleges " . . . must lay the foundation for wise citizenship." Again: "About all that we can say today is that the one certain calling [for all people] is citizenship." As for coherent college curricula, Hutchins wrote: "So-called colleges of liberal arts, in which only the name survives, announce that the student is liberally educated when he has accumulated 120 semester hours of miscellaneous credits in his account book."

A majority of Americans may believe in God, or whatever they might call transcendent energy and intelligence, but our society is, in fact, driven by forces antithetic to the idea of anything transcending phenomena. Lacking an idea of God or cosmic intelligence, the life of the universe becomes simply the play of physical and chemical forces. Consequently the individual life can be no more than an arbitrary arrangement of events, one strung out after another, and the only meaning any human life has is whatever the individual gives it.

Since there is no objective meaning to human existence, society can aim no higher than to preserve itself. But how can society preserve itself when virtue or the virtues cannot be discussed among the self-described intellectual élite? How can it preserve itself if it cannot agree on the intellectual skills citizenship demands?

Despite this, the typical liberal arts college offers a boilerplate justification for itself: it claims to train students to think independently and critically: it claims it leads them to examine their own biases. In other words, it claims to develop free men and women, and claims to accomplish this by developing one fragment of the person—reason.

But becoming a free man or woman takes far more hard work (and work of a different kind) than any college can offer. Our colleges are capable of developing reason, but it is reason lacking understanding and imagination. Technical education produces graduates with this bare reason, and does it admirably, producing engineers, designers, architects, and experts in cybernetics. But reason of this kind is mechanical thinking, the sort of thinking a computer performs efficiently. Mechanical thinking builds skyscrapers and giant cities with rings of suburbs, drains oil from the earth, sheers off mountaintops for coal, and demands new machines of every kind, including instruments of universal destruction.

The people who design the techniques and operations that dehumanize our environment are not free men and women. They are servants of an automaton over which no one has control. The rage of students in the sixties against this automaton vaporized with time, and they, like the communards, were absorbed back into the System they had raged against.

NINE
New Canaan Revisited

Graduated from Columbia University I returned home to New Canaan, knowing I would stay only long enough to earn the money I needed to go back on the road. New Canaan had provided me with a thorough education in the thoughts and ways of American upper class bourgeoisie.

This economic group—America's dominant class of the 1960s, which was well represented by New Canaan—had no lack of shared beliefs. New Canaan housed a culture that was nurtured in other towns across America where well-to-do white Protestants gathered. Highly competitive, elitist, and focused on money, New Canaanites might look smugly and disdainfully, and sometimes fearfully, on those who lived outside their small enclave. New Canaanites were fortunate indeed, and knew it, for they proclaimed their town to be "the next station to Heaven."

Blacks, Jews and Mediterranean peoples were thought to belong to a lower order. Genteel Protestants could scoff at blacks at cocktail parties, and could even joke about Martin Luther King's assassination. A few days after King was assassinated, at home from Columbia University, I stood in a group of New Canaan men at a cocktail party as they nursed their drinks. One in a hearty voice said to another, "You made it back fast from Memphis." The others laughed. That was a good joke.

The Civil Rights struggles disrupted white people of all kinds everywhere, for where might equal rights and enfranchisement lead? Blacks like Stokey Carmichael and Malcolm X were feared and hated.

All of the exclusivity felt and practiced by monied Protestants in New Canaan and in other enclaves of genteel white, Anglo-Saxon Protestants is nothing new to humanity. In the case of New Canaan, exclusivity was in partnership with competition.

My brother-in-law, who played on New Canaan High School's varsity football team, said that he and his teammates were told that if they won, they could shake hands with the opposition—otherwise not. New Canaan, he said, was "competition run amuck."

His eldest daughter, who attended New Canaan High School, said that girls exchanged notes in class, making fun of any girl who wore the same dress more than once in two weeks.

But competition, whether in sports or business or any endeavor, implies fear. Competition, which is a hallmark of an individualistic society, is one in which fear dominates. The fear is often subtle, and the person it motivates is often unaware of the motivation. As our society continues fragmenting, its members flying off centrifugally beyond any communal center, fear increases until, as today, Americans are divided into many hostile camps.

To be sure, I met some decent adult men in New Canaan, and remember them fondly. But the ones that return to my mind unbidden are the angry ones. The anger simmered below the surface but could flame out unexpectedly. Perhaps someone took too much time doing the New Canaanite's bidding, or refused to do it.

The most dramatic display of white Anglo-Saxon Protestant anger I witnessed came the evening I was returning to New Canaan from Columbia on one of the many trains that left Grand Central in the early evening. Gate after gate had signs listing the suburban towns each train serviced. The floor of the great building with its immensely high ceiling was mobbed with men wearing suits and carrying briefcases, moving quickly in all directions across the floor.

I boarded my train and found a seat at the back of a car,

next to the door. The train rumbled as it idled beside the platform. A conductor punched the tickets of the men in the seat beside me. The door behind me opened slowly and a commuter, a New York executive, staggered inside. He stepped in back of the conductor and said, "Hey!"

The conductor turned.

The drunk said, "I'm back."

"Get off."

The conductor turned the drunk around, pulled open the door and pushed him onto the platform at the car's end. The door closed behind them. The train began moving and a moment later the conductor was back in the car. Once again he bent over, punching a ticket for a man in the seat ahead of me. The door opened and the drunk executive re-entered. He came behind the conductor, lifted a hand, and brought a cigarette down on the conductor's neck.

The conductor yelped, straightened and turned. He slugged the drunk, who fell to the floor. The drunken commuter staggered to his feet. The conductor opened the door again and pushed the drunk out ahead of himself. The door closed behind them. Minutes later the conductor returned and resumed punching tickets. He went into the car ahead.

Soon after, the drunk re-appeared, his clothes askew, staggering more than before.

"He really wiped the floor with me," he announced to the car.

***

Spending much of my adolescence in New Canaan prepared me for the rise to power of corporatists within our government. For as the wealth of corporate managers increased alarmingly, so did their control of each sector of our economy. As that control increased, so did their presence in our Federal government. One after another, men of high corporate rank were appointed to cabinet positions within one administration after another. These were men who did not brook dissent within their corporations, and they could not brook it when in government.

They knew how to handle workers. They knew how to

handle citizens of a Republic—and slowly the Republic ceased to exist. As one of their tools read from his script, "Either you are for us or against us."

PART THREE

ONE
Return to Santa Fe (fall 1968)

Several hundred of us stood in the gymnasium stripped down to our shorts. Those around me, and all those I had seen and heard, were working class kids. They would twist around to joke with someone in back of them. They bent forward and laughed when they told one another they wanted "to shoot one of the little gooks." Today I am not sure if this was bluff or if they really wanted to be a part of the war. I did not talk with them, and I did not want to serve with them. I did not want to go to Vietnam.

I thought often about the war. Months earlier my attitude had changed from one of uncertainty to one of outright opposition. Now every evening I watched television news and saw American troops threading through jungle or caught in firefights. I saw footage of men running under fire for the body of one of their platoon and dragging it back. Every night we saw more wounded, more dead.

Why were Americans dying in Vietnam? Authorities told us that once the communists seized Vietnam that Cambodia, Laos, and Thailand would be overrun. Japan would fall next and soon our allies in the Pacific would fall under communist control. This was the "domino theory." State Department officials, generals and politicians proclaimed the theory on television and over radio and soon everyone from briefcase-carrying businessmen to housewives believed it.

And while perhaps hundreds of thousands of young middle-class boys defied the values of post-war America and found draft deferments, working class youth volunteered or were drafted for the war. As a working class poet friend said, "The Vietnam War was fought by the working class. For the middle class, the sixties were one big party."

At St. John's we had read and discussed Plato's dialogue, *The Crito*. This dialogue takes place in a prison cell where Socrates is held by fellow Athenians who have condemned him to death. His friends outline a plan of escape, but Socrates argues against flight. He imagines the laws speaking to him, saying that through them his parents were married and he was born and educated. The laws say that by fleeing you, Socrates, will be helping to destroy us. You had seventy years to leave Athens but chose to stay. You, of all men, understand the implicit contract between yourself and us. If everyone chose to obey the laws only when they saw fit, chaos would follow.

I could not accept Socrates' argument, for when laws are manifestly unjust, re-establishing justice involves much risk. We Americans had powerful examples to support this, not the least the American Revolution. We had another, very recent example, that of civil disobedience that won civil rights legislation for black Americans and had gotten one of their leaders assassinated.

I was not a conscientious objector and would have fought the war if America had been threatened, but I did not believe in the domino theory. I would not be made part of another machine. I did wonder if I was shirking my obligation to America, but finally I decided I would move to Canada.

I visited with one of my Bentley teachers at the Biltmore Bar in New York to say goodbye. He said that if I did not go someone would have to take my place, perhaps die in my place. That did not make sense. The person who was tapped to take my place would also have the choice to leave.

I told my parents my plan. My mother pleaded with me not to go.

"I won't be able to see you again."

"Sure you will."

"You don't know anyone there."

"I'll make friends."

"How can you leave this country? This is your country. This is America."

"I don't want to live here anymore."

"If you go to Canada I won't be able to face my friends in the bridge club. They'll know you turned un-American and fled." That is what it came down to—not losing face with her friends in the bridge club.

"Do your bit for Uncle Sam."

"Mom, I might get killed."

"No, you won't."

Father, on the other hand, was more philosophical. He said, "Think this over carefully. It means never coming back to this country again."

I knew that was right, yet I still packed a suitcase. I would first go to Santa Fe, say goodbye to friends, and then head north. On my way to Santa Fe I would stop in Chicago to see Sean Fitzpatrick.

I took a train to New York and there boarded a bus for Chicago. I found Sean living with a girlfriend. and drinking heavily. The words, 'DON'T DRINK I LOVE YOU" were written on their apartment wall in big red letters. Sean had tried covering the letters with a coat of white paint but the coat was thin and the words showed through.

I stayed with them two days. Sean persuaded me to trade my suitcase for his duffle bag. A bag, he said, would make it easier traveling on freights. During my two days in Chicago we toured the botanical gardens and the Field Museum. I studied road atlases in the Loyola University library, determined to hop freights all the way to Santa Fe. One U.S. atlas showed that the nearest cluster of rails leading to the Southwest was in Joliet, south of Chicago.

The day before I left, Sean took us to a bar and bought drinks. After the second drink, when he urged a third, he seemed to be smirking. "You want to get him drunk," his girlfriend said and Sean laughed nastily.

The next day Sean and his girlfriend came with me to the bus station. I bought a ticket and checked my duffle bag and we cut across the street to a bar for a last minute beer before shaking hands in front of the bus. "Wolf wants to make a big deal out of this," Sean said. He was more cynical than he had been in Santa Fe. Something mean had emerged in Sean. It was an uncomfortable moment and forced on both sides. It was the last I ever saw of him.

As the bus roared south on a narrow two-lane highway, I wondered if I would have trouble finding the Joliet freight yards. The bus was a local, and the driver knew his riders. He talked and joked with them as we stopped in an endless series of small towns.

Dark clouds loomed overhead. We splashed through small pools and puddles from yesterday's rain. I pictured myself walking midnight Joliet streets looking for a cheap hotel. Even though I had 300 dollars in my pocket I was reluctant to spend any of it. Overhead it looked as though hell would break loose, and I did not have a slicker. I felt my trip was doomed.

We entered the outskirts of a city that I was sure was Joliet. Sometimes we crossed railroad tracks and sometimes paralleled them. In downtown Joliet we crossed under a cluster of tracks and I wondered if I should get off. We drove another mile and passed under a railroad bridge. I pulled the cord.

I hauled my duffle bag up a dirt embankment, hoping no one spotted me. The sun smeared the horizon a violent red. A dozen tracks spread out before me. I followed them away from town, with woods on one side and warehouses on the other.

"BLAAAH!" A Santa Fe locomotive blared its whistle, hauling a line of freight cars down the tracks, headed my way. Before it sped past I stepped closer to the tracks. As the caboose roared by I saw a brakeman leaning out the window. At the last moment, as he was hurled alongside me, I threw up an arm and above the tremendous rattling of the wheels yelled, "Where's the yard?" He smiled and waved an arm, pointing in the direction the train had come. I waved back.

Suddenly I realized that on the embankment I could be seen from nearby streets. Twice I heard sirens and thought I had been spotted.

Ahead of me tracks diverged in several directions; I moved straight ahead. By then I had walked several miles but still my energy was high from the thought of hopping a freight and from the feeling that freights give me of American rawness and power. By now it was dark and bright lights atop high poles illuminated an acre of tracks and a huge railroad bridge spanning the river to my right. Rows of boxcars and tankers lay ahead, but no engines. A shack with lights sat in the middle of the yard.

I was beat. I wanted to lie down but thought if I did not push on I might miss the next freight west and have to wait another day.

Another train roared as it approached. I was thirty feet from the track when a Santa Fe passenger train hurtled by in a clatter and slam of wheels and springs, throwing a gust of wind so strong it knocked me backwards, staggering. I stood holding the duffle bag, gawking, feeling the vastness of the country and wondering if anyone aside from the conductor and engineer was awake and would see and envy me, wishing that he too were loafing across country.

I trudged towards the shack. Car lights and men with lanterns moved slowly towards me. I thought, "It's the cops. I've been spotted."

I ran for the bushes to my left, dove in and looked out. The men were still coming. I scrambled down a gully and hid behind bushes to wait them out. I waited until I felt they had passed and resumed walking toward the shack.

I heard another train moving slowly towards me. I looked between two boxcars. I did not know if the approaching train was still being made up or heading out; I did not care where it went, I just wanted out. I climbed a coupling between boxcars and as the train crawled past I clutched the grab irons on a coal car. My heavy bag dragged me down, almost pulling me off. The train stopped and a switchman with a lamp approached. Embarrassed, I got off and asked if this was heading west.

"Yep," he said, "Kansas City."

"When does it leave?"

"Bout two this morning."

"Anything going further west?"

"Where you headed?"

"Santa Fe."

"You'll have to take this, then transfer in Kansas City. You've got a long wait before this is ready. Might as well stay in the shack."

"Thanks."

We ambled to the shack I had seen earlier. He set the lamp down on a table. It was a small shack, one room with a table and chairs, calendars, schedules, pinups, papers stuck to the walls, and a few lamps. It smelled of oil and grease.

"You can sleep here till the train pulls out. Sack out on the table."

He removed papers and cups from the top.

"There's a shower here,' he said, moving to one end of the shack and pointing. "We got towels here."

"Thanks a lot."

"I'll be back when it's made up so you can take off." He disappeared into the night.

I stretched out on the table but could not sleep with the slamming of the cars. I unpacked my bag, took out a change of clothes and took a shower and slept. When I awoke hours later, the air was damp. I felt a bit dazed but wandered out in the dark because now other railroaders were outside the shack, sitting on benches. I sat and talked to them. My friend came back to say he had lined me up a car, told me the car number and the track it was on. When I accompanied him beyond the hearing of others he told me he had routed it all the way to Santa Fe.

"Only don't tell anybody anywhere else," he said, "or I'm in trouble. The train's heading out of here later than I thought, 'bout six this morning."

Back in the shack I slept some more. When the eastern rim shown pink, I headed for my train, crossing over couplings and walking until I found my car. I cleared a stretch of planking and found cardboard among clumps of grass. I rolled out my sleeping bag on the cardboard and lay down.

The train was still slamming back and forth, adding more cars. By the time it was ready the sky was light and the yard was silent. I hopped out of my boxcar to walk forward and see the engine when suddenly the engine roared and WOMP! the freight started up, lurching a million tons of steel after it. Then CLUNK! it slowed with the weight. Everything stopped. Then WOMP! the train started pulling out with a clanking of one car after another.

At first I thought more cars were being added but the train kept moving; I realized it was leaving the yard. I took off running against the direction of the train, hoping to get to my boxcar before it moved too fast for me to hop on. By the time I saw it, the freight was clipping along. I had to reverse direction and run alongside my boxcar, heave my bag in, throw my hands onto the car floor and still running, leap—upward and forward—not knowing if I could jump far enough. I smashed my groin against the steel edge with stabbing pain and hauled myself in, off again across America.

We were moving faster and faster, cruising over the ground I had covered the night before. Jazz symphonies crashed in my mind to the syncopated smashing of springs and wheels. I sat on the edge of the boxcar or sometimes leaned against the open door, watching the soft southern Illini plains, the gentle butter-in-your-mouth softness of the grass putting me in mind of the time I rode past another pasture at dawn to see horses chomping grass in the mist. I had nothing to do but relax, singing every song that came into my head.

That night I rolled out my sleeping bag, cushioning my head against the jarring car as we hurtled south, passing through name-less towns, still afraid the train would stop and a yard cop would find me. But I dropped off and slept until dawn. The next day we traveled again through prairie. I was becoming bored.

The yardman had said this freight was stopping in Kansas City. The second day about dusk we rolled into a city—first scattered buildings, then warehouses, brickworks and factories and more buildings tumbling into great masses. With tracks converging and paralleling, it dawned on me that maybe this was Kansas City.

It was dark. I was hoping the train would not stop and leave me stranded. It did stop. I waited ten minutes, twenty minutes, a half hour. No movement. It was not putting on cars.

"Well," I thought, "This is Kansas City," and hopped off. I did not want to spend another day or two in an empty boxcar, even if it did take me to Santa Fe. I would take the road instead.

But as soon as I walked a half-mile from the track, the freight started. This was not Kansas City, Kansas but Kansas City, Missouri! As I watched the freight leave, I felt lonesome and de-flated. Now I had to hitchhike miles through a city.

I lumbered up a grade and over a fence to the highway where cars whizzed by. Luckily I got a ride from an old man and his son heading a few miles down the road. They were interested in what I was doing and I jabbered on about the freight ride and Santa Fe. My next lift came from two teenagers on a kick.

"Where ya goin"?"

"Santa Fe, New Mexico."

"Got yourself a long trip."

"You bet."

"Well us, we're just out cruising along. Got any timetable?"

"Nope."

"Come along."

"Sure nuf. Where you headed?"

"Get some drinks and girls."

"Right by me."

We went off across Kansas City, lights and cars flashing by as we sped off the highway onto city streets.

The kid in the passenger seat said, "Like a drink?"

"Sure."

He passed me a pint of whiskey.

"Okay," I said to myself. "This is okay."

We roared out of the city onto a county highway, looking for the tavern where girls were supposed to meet them. When we found the tavern we hung around and had a few beers, but the girls never showed.

Back in the car the driver said, "What's your pleasure? You wanta get back on the road or you wanta bunk at our place? We'll give ya a ride to a bus in the morning."

"Well, I'd like to stay with you."

"No problem."

They lived in a wood-frame building in a working class neighborhood. Inside, everything was thrown about. I rolled out my sleeping bag on the living room floor amid the clutter. The next morning I was chipper but the boys were quiet and hung over. They invited me to look them up the next time I was in Kansas City. Since I had decided to take a bus to Amarillo instead of hitchhiking, the boys dropped me off at a bus stop on their way to work.

"The bus will get you to the bus station downtown," they told me.

Inside the terminal I bought a ticket to Pampa, Texas and sat on a bench watching a tall man in jeans and western hat move about. He reminded me very much of Gene West. He was lean and sunburnt, a workingman and sure of himself: I could see it in his gestures and the way he moved. When he sat down I got up and sat next to him. I asked him where he was going.

"Denver," he said.

We began a conversation that continued on the bus. He asked me if I wanted a job working construction in Colorado. I would have said yes if my mind had not been set on Santa Fe and Canada. He gave me his name and address in Denver. He said he was later going to Florida on work but the invitation was still open.

I got to Pampa at night. On the street I asked a man for a hotel and he gave me the name of an old style Texas hotel with veranda and porch. The next morning I was up early. As I stood on the veranda looking on the deserted street I watched an old man in blue jeans and Stetson come ambling along. Suddenly he began yelling and leaping and waving. I thought he was crazy, or drunk, or both. I thought he ought to keep out of sight before he was locked up. While I stood and stared, I realized he was yelling at me! He jumped some more. He would go into a crouch and leap, waving his arms in a great halleluiah. He was joyed to see me. I realized he was alone in town and my duffle bag showed him a fellow traveler. I was not sure whether I was pleased or not, but crossed the street to see him.

"Damn," he said, "you ever see a town like this? Where you from? I been here in Pampa the last two days and I ain't seen nothing like it ever! Sphewww! Damn! Where you headed?"

"Santa Fe."

His eyes widened. "Yeah? Santy Fee. Passed through there once. Damn! Whenever I think of the miles I've put on these feet my brain nearly passes out I get so hot. Know what I mean? Wheeew! Sons of bitches here'd rather shoot you than look at ya.

Forgit yer hungry, these bastids ain't gonna feed ya 'er give ya a nickel or the powder t' blow you t'hell, that's about it. When I git outa this town mister I'm gonna be happy. Hap-eee!"

All the while he talked he looked around, swinging his body about, craning his head quickly in one direction, then another.

"Where you headed?" I asked.

"Dallas. Home."

I nodded.

He looked at me askance. "Yeah, that's where I live. Belong. Goin' back. Ain't been there in two years. DAMN my feet is sore."

He jumped up and down.

"How do I get to the highway?"

He pointed. "Down there, keep goin'. You'll see the signs."

"Take care."

"Say hello to Santy Fee for me."

I walked to the highway. The air was warming up; the sun was on my face. Cars whipped by. A kid gave me a ride 100 miles down the road to Tucumcari on Route 66 where I got a lift from a salesman who took me another 100 miles on 66 to Clines Corners. There I picked up a ride from a hefty black man who knew some of my friends and gave me a ride to Santa Fe; in fact he dropped me off in front of Hal West's studio.

I walked inside. Hal, sitting behind his table said, "Hell, kid, we weren't expecting you back."

I shook Hal's hand, grinned, and sat down.

"Make us both a toddy, Bob."

"All right."

I poured the drinks and said, "'Let's have a game of dominoes."

Hal dumped the box of bones on the table and we turned them over, plain sides up.

"I haven't played dominoes in a year," I said.

We each picked seven bones.

"It's good to see you, son."

"It's good to see you, Hal."

I was back home, back with Hal.

TWO
Santa Fe (1968-69)

Seeing all of Hal's belongings—down to the green felt pad on which he laid his watch—placed just as they had been a year ago was a comfort. So was Hal's slow drawl.

After a game of dominoes I asked him, "Do you mind if I call Alan?"

"Anything you want, Bob. I haven't seen Alan in a long time."

I called and in a few minutes Alan came through the back door and pumped my hand.

This was one of those late September afternoons, lazy and peaceful, like it mostly was at Hal's, a world unto itself. We played dominoes and listened to Jimmy Rodger's songs of trains, hoboes, and two-timing women.

"This is your senior year? I asked Alan.

"It would be. When Gail and the kids came this summer I took a job teaching math at Santa Fe Prep. Do you have a place to stay?"

"No."

"Stay with us."

"Thanks."

"What are your plans?"

"I got my draft notice. I'm heading for Canada and came to say good-bye."

"They need another math teacher at prep. I'll introduce you to the headmaster."

Now, suddenly, teaching was a possibility! I had not expected this. If I taught, I might not have to start a new life in Canada.

Later Alan drove me to his house, littered with baby blankets, books, papers, toys—a pandemonium replete with whining children.

The next day he took me to Santa Fe Prep and introduced me to the headmaster, Mr. Reynolds. Santa Fe Prep had been good for Alan. He clearly liked teaching and was serious about it, and clearly Mr. Reynolds respected Alan. I liked the school and Mr. Reynolds and wanted to teach there.

I wanted to increase my chance of getting a teaching job, and that same day I called the New Mexico Department of Education. The day after I interviewed with the man who issued the state's emergency teaching certificates. He had an opening for a seventh and eighth grade math teacher in Espanola, twenty-five miles north of Santa Fe. He wanted to know if I could handle the classroom and I told him of my recent trip and the time I rode through the L.A. yards and of Billy the Red. He offered me the job.

The very next day Mr. Reynolds called me at Hal's as I was playing dominoes and offered me the position at Prep. I told him that I had already made a verbal agreement with the state, and Mr. Reynolds said he would have to withdraw his offer.

Meanwhile, life at Alan's home was frantic. Gail lurched about with seemingly random movements. Her hair was straggly and her attempts to fix it, pushing it out of her face with a gentle motion, was as haphazard as her attempts to keep order in her life and in the house. She did dishes, washed clothes, hung the clothes on lines, cleaned baby bottles, fed the kids—an impossible routine as long Alan stumbled in her way or sat and read.

When the boys ran and yelled and Gail called Alan for help, Alan would say, "Hey, you brats! You better watch it!" or "Hey! Stop that!" I never saw Alan play with the children.

The boys dragged their blankets through rooms and dropped them anywhere. Unwashed dishes lay in the sink. Alan left books and papers on the floor, on chairs, on tables. Once I watched Gail, haggard from endless work, holding clothespins in her mouth while hanging the wash, struggling to pin a sheet while the boys stumbled over her. She called Alan for help and Alan yelled from his living room chair, "Leave mommy alone and come back inside." The boys kept pestering Gail, ignoring her yells. At last she screamed, "Alan! . . . DO something!"

Alan stood, stomped awkwardly across the room and out the back door. "What do you want me to do?" he shouted. "I called for the kids! They don't listen to me." The boys continued whining.

In those days I could not see why Gail did not discipline the boys and leave Alan to his studies. I thought she was simply incapable of keeping order.

Clearly I could not stay there. I found a small adobe—a studio converted from an old garage that once belonged to the writer, Max Eastman. Leon Green had been renting it when I first met Gene, and I later learned that another friend had also lived there.

***

Several weeks after I rented the casita, I went with Gail, Alan, and their children to the bar in La Fonda. Alan and I talked while Gail minded the boys. At first the boys merely chattered, but in time they became bored and started tottering around our table. They paid no attention to Gail. She became as agitated as the boys while Alan and I continued talking.

"Alan, let's go," Gail said.

Alan ignored her. The boys continued crabbing at each other and tottering around our table.

"Peter, stop it!" Gail commanded the oldest boy, grabbing him by the arm. "Alan, let's go!" Gail repeated.

Alan continued to talk. The boys continued crabbing at each other.

Gail jumped up. "That's it, Alan. Don't come home tonight or ANY night from now on!" She grabbed the boys by the arms.

Alan said nothing as Gail walked across the bar. When she disappeared he said, "This has been coming for a long time."

I told Alan, "You can stay with me."

That night Alan moved into my casita. We took the mattress off the bed and Alan slept on that while I slept on the box springs. Between the few furnishings in the casita—the bed, the mattress, the bookcase and gas heater—the entire floor was almost covered. Slowly Alan's papers and books covered what was left.

In the mornings Alan and I left for work. In the afternoons we met and cooked dinner. The kitchen was just large enough for one person. The sink began filling up with dirty dishes, pots, knives and forks, cups and glasses. The sink looked bad; so did the sideboard covered with more dirty plates, pots, knives forks and bits of food. I told Alan, "We better eat off paper plates." So we did. In the first few days when we finished a meal we dumped the paper plates in a brown grocery bag along with the empty tin cans and milk cartons. Soon one brown bag with garbage became two brown bags with garbage. Then three. Cheap ceramic plates had not been our problem.

***

At Espanola Junior High not only did I have to learn to pronounce Spanish names—those I had heard in Duran I remembered—I had to teach myself what was called the new math. This was a way of teaching mathematics from its foundations. This meant abandoning the base ten system, the system we use in everyday life. We had exercises translating from one base into others and performing arithmetic operations in other systems. All of this was new to me, as it was to the students, and at first I spent evenings in my casita studying.

I bought a car with an unsecured loan and commuted to Espanola from Santa Fe in a car pool with four other teachers. One of them, Anthony Trujillo, was also a math teacher. Anthony taught across the hall from me. Anthony, who was short and balding, had a heavy Spanish accent and wore thick plastic glass frames. I learned about paddling students from Anthony when he knocked on my classroom door and asked me if I would witness a paddling. A young child stood in the hall and watched us as Anthony gripped a wide paddle in one hand. "Turn around and grab your knees," Anthony told the youngster. The child bent over and Anthony whacked him once on the rear. "Thank you, Mr. Wolf," Anthony said and opened the door for the student.

I doubt I ever had a good reason to paddle a student, but occasionally I did, just to make sure nothing ever got out of hand. I would knock on Anthony's door and ask for his paddle and ask him to accompany me outside. None of the students ever complained to their parents. Had Anthony and I done this thirty years later we would have seen the inside of a courtroom. Forty years after Espanola, when I was back in Santa Fe, I asked Anthony why he paddled his students. "Because they used to make fun of me," he said.

For the next two years I taught general math and algebra to the very gentle children of this nondescript town in a land of bare, dry earth. I wanted to be a good teacher, but my heart was not in it. I was adequate, I hope, but no more. My mind was fixed on writing and for the life that came after three-thirty every weekday afternoon.

That fall, on one jaunt to a used bookstore, whose entrance was in the patio of a centuries old compound, I found a copy of *The Lady's Not for Burning*, a verse comedy by the English playwright Christopher Fry. I had never heard of Fry before, and here inside this yellow-covered book was a packet of articles on Fry, along with photographs of this nattily dressed Englishman who loved tweeds. His play was intoxicating, his language meteoric. I, too, would write verse comedies with language that popped and burst like roman candles.

Fry and his language became the center of my Imaginative life. I memorized entire scenes and would declaim them to anyone who would listen. I, too, wanted to write brilliant verse dramas, see them staged on Broadway, and live like a gentleman in a country cottage just like Fry.

THREE
Santa Fe Then and Now

My casita was a short walk from Claude's bar on Canyon Road, which ran its crooked, narrow way up into the mountain foothills. Many of Santa Fe's artists and writers rented small adobe homes and studios clustered on or near Canyon Road. After Alan moved in with me, we spent most evenings at Claude's, which was the gathering place for Santa Fe's bohemian colony.

Since the early decades of the 1900s, Santa Fe had been a magnet for artists of the caliber of John Sloan and Randall Davy and for writers like Mary Austin, Paul Horgan and Oliver La-Farge. As these men and women died, others took their place. By the mid-sixties Claude's bar had become the social center for this colony. Claude's was an expression of the energy of the sixties, and for me it was the most notable node of sixties energy in Santa Fe.

In hindsight we who came of age in the sixties know that period to have been not only one of civil and social turmoil, but of enormous creative energy.

For my part, I hoped through my traveling and meetings across the country to create a documentary record of late twentieth century America. I wrote fast spontaneous accounts of travels and meetings, but my deepest passion lay in the theater. I had written plays for the Tiffany melodrama and was now writing a verse comedy that I hoped to be as witty as the comedies of Fry or Shaw. My plan was to draft my plays in Santa Fe, have them performed there, and, as I said, move on to New York.

I was very much aware of the creative energy that thrummed throughout America in the sixties. Whatever its source, it would not have been sustained without a thriving economy and cheap food and rent, all of which make possible a creative life for the young. But what was the meaning of the collective life of the artists and writers who clustered about Canyon Road or anywhere else in the country? What was the significance of the country's creative explosion? In the film, *My Dinner with Andre,* theater director Andre Gregory tells writer Wallace Shawn that he thinks the sixties were the last great upsurge of the human spirit. In retrospect, this seems correct.

The youthful idealism of the sixties died slowly, with one assassination after another. Then during Reagan's administration, when avarice was called the grease that sustained American business and therefore American prosperity, youth understood that public service was time wasted that could be better spent earning an MBA. At the same time, Santa Fe became chic and fashionable. Real estate values vaulted skyward. As older artists, or grocery store owners, or small retail shop owners on Canyon Road died or retired, their homes, shops and studios were turned into commercial art galleries for tourists.

Many of Santa Fe's artists, not able to afford Canyon Road rentals, dispersed to other towns; the rest scattered across the city.

The synergy that came from that cluster of creative people was gone. In 1980, when I returned for a visit I was stunned: the old city had been taken by the scruff of its neck, shaken, washed, painted and varnished. And its bohemian sub-culture had vanished.

FOUR
Claude's Bar (1968-1970)

On a sun-filled afternoon following my return, Alan and I stood at Claude's with our backs to the front window feeling the warm sunlight that flooded the room. We were thinking of the summer of 1966, the year of melodramas and Hal and our nights at the Palace Restaurant. Before I went to live at Marlene's, so much had been good that summer. Alan and Mac and I would leave on a moment's notice to explore some town or to visit someone we might have met only the day before. "That," said Alan, "was a golden summer."

Try as I might, I could not recreate it, even at Claude's where painters, writers, and loafers, Indians and Anglos clustered. There was Paul Kramer, a pop artist who claimed to be a black belt and told me his hands were registered but was missing his two upper front teeth; Eli Levin, a New York transplant and a fine social realist painter; David Briggs, a flamenco guitarist; Beverly Mc-Crary and Hannah Hibbs, older students at the College of Santa Fe who ran with the Hollywood crowd when it was in town. Older painters like Hal West and Jim Morris occasionally still came, so did teachers at the Santa Fe Indian School. Stan Noyes, author of the respected novel, *No Flowers for a Clown*, appeared occasionally, as did Hal West's son, Jerry, who developed into one of New Mexico's most accomplished artists.

Then there were the loungers. They confirmed each other's gifts, propped each other up, accepted and encouraged each other's illusions.

The nightlife at Claude's was intense with its varnished front bar glinting under the lights and lined with souls that were searching . . .

A few of the drinkers, like the gaunt-faced and bearded Finn O'Hara, I saw only once or twice. O'Hara belonged to the class of customers that had the status of legends. Some of Claude's drinkers spoke of these legends in awe, almost in whispers. Most of the legends were dead, like Alfred Morang, who had painted small scenes on the walls of a dangerous bar just down the street. Others had once been Claude's regulars but now drifted in and out of town. These characters, as I say, were spoken of almost in whispers, as though they lived in a mythical past and we, pitiful by comparison, lived in ordinary times.

From what I heard Claude's loungers say of him, Finn O'Hara's name invoked an image of a dangerous man, a walking time bomb. He was said to have chewed a glass at the bar one night. Had he swallowed any of the glass? Even supposing O'Hara had done so, it could not have cut his mouth or stomach. Such did not happen to legends.

One of Claude's regulars who later became a prominent New Mexico lawyer, had just passed his bar exam and was drinking at Claude's the night before his first job out of law school, clerking for a federal judge. Sometime during the night he passed out. The bar was crowded and noisy and no one noticed him lying on the floor. None of the employees noticed him when they closed up. When Claude's opened the next morning my friend headed to the judge's chambers where the judge's secretary told him to go home and sleep it off.

Another of Claude's regulars was John Hanson, a dedicated abstract artist. I met Hanson through Hal West on the first night that Hal and I visited Claude's in the summer of 1966. Claude's was Hanson's second home. Hanson was Alan's height, about six foot four inches and solidly built. He was raised in Maine and had lived in Santa Fe periodically since the early sixties. In 1966 he returned to settle in Santa Fe. Hanson had a deep, booming voice that intimidated some people. He was a heavy drinker and when drunk he seemed ready to explode. He could drink steadily for five or six hours and wake the next morning with no hangover and hike five miles into the mountains.

I stepped back to the bar.

"I heard you call Tweedledum an adolescent schmuck."

"Yes, I did," Hanson insisted. "And with good reason."

"That was very bad manners," I told him.

"Listen, buddy, my manners are impeccable. My mother brought me up with very good manners."

It was easy to get Hanson riled if you knew which buttons to push.

"Don't shout," I said.

"I'll shout if I damn well please."

"What do you mean you have good manners? You've been shouting in my ears for the last two months."

"Yes," Hanson shouted, "that's right."

"That's boorish," I countered.

"Yes! You're damn RIGHT it's boorish."

"Then you're a liar."

"Don't call me a liar! I am NOT a LIAR!"

"Either you're a liar or you're mistaken. You just said you had good manners and now you tell me you're a boor."

"He's right," Alan told Hanson.

"You two"—Hanson paused, then hissed—"are half-wits." He smiled.

***

Hanson was a perpetual presence at Claude's after five o'clock. Before he began drinking at five, he would be friendly and willing to show his paintings to any interested person. I visited his little adobe numerous times and John would offer coffee and pull out his latest work. In those days they were large, abstract paintings of the New England seacoast, painted in small patches of color.

Hanson, I gathered from one dark painting of an army brig, had a quarrel with army discipline and had gone AWOL or been otherwise frequently insubordinate. Whatever the case, he been thrown into the brig where he had broken down: his mind had fractured there and he still dreaded the memory of the brig and his breakdown. The dark core was still in Hanson and he feared it.

Hanson lived off a trust fund and so was able to devote himself to painting, drinking and hiking. Others in the Canyon Road colony had neither painting, nor writing, nor any other art through which they might have staved off self-destruction. One of these, Pete Townsend, became one of Claude's habitués. I met Townsend soon after my return from New York at The Forge, a downtown Santa Fe bar. Hal and I were sitting at a table at one end of The Forge, looking at a man sitting by himself at the bar. The man wore a brown sports jacket and thin tie and had close-cropped hair. Hal said, "That's Pete Townsend." I caught the scorn in Hal's voice.

Pete looked in our direction, saw us and came over.

"Good evening, Hal," he said, holding his drink in one hand and extending the other. Hal looked at the extended hand, then slowly stretched out his own, but did not ask Pete to join us. I noticed that Pete's face was just beginning to sag. His jowls were fleshy and his eyes puffy, with bags beneath them. His clothes were ten, twenty years out of fashion. His jacket collar was too narrow, so was his tie. He dressed carefully; his gestures were tight. I came to see that this was how Townsend tried to cover a disintegrating interior.

In the coming weeks as I visited Claude's I was to get to know Townsend, which opened another chapter in my life, and not an innocent one, but thankfully brief.

Soon after I met Townsend at The Forge, I saw him again at Claude's. Townsend was urbane and intelligent. He had written advertising copy in New York, or so he said. I was drawn into his life. Our relationship cemented at Claude's where we met to drink and play pool.

The poolroom at Claude's—a small side room usually crowded with loungers and lit by overhead neon lights—was intense with loud talk and the jukebox in the next room. There may have been one good player among the scores that played that table, but most, like Townsend, thought themselves good, if not expert. They were loud and fed one another with mutual praise.

As fall passed into winter 1969, Claude's grew in intensity. In those alcohol-fueled nights, Claude's was a howl of activity in this—the heyday of its life. Great crowds roiled about; bodies danced in the side room, men crammed together at the bar while couples sat at tables by the fireplace in the back room.

In our first conversations Townsend told me that he not only was a writer but that he had a New York agent, Mary Bradley. I was impressed. Townsend said that many years ago there had been three young stars on the American literary horizon, "There was Norman Mailer . . . Irwin Shaw . . . and me." I believed him. Townsend would then say, "I could have been a contender," imitating Marlon Brando in *On the Waterfront*. Townsend quoted that line frequently.

I believed him. After all, he had published one or two short stories, which he showed me. I do not remember anything about them. Certainly they showed promise— no doubt about that—because New York's literary establishment predicted a brilliant future for him. I did not ask him what had happened. The breaks had simply not fallen his way and he had gone into advertising. Here in Santa Fe then was a writer who had not only published and had a New York agent, but had a mysterious, tragic past. He was my friend, and my drinking buddy!

I handed Pete a copy of *Lucrezia*, a verse drama I had written after the style of Christopher Fry. I sat with Pete as he read it, and watched with great pleasure as he would suddenly say, "My God! This is great stuff!" put down the manuscript and stare into space.

I was greatly impressed and began to think myself another Christopher Fry, or better yet, Christopher Marlowe. Pete encouraged these fantasies. He said, "This is as good as Fry," and he himself professed a love for *The Lady's Not for Burning*, parts of which I would declaim for him.

In the autumn of 1968 I was trying to recreate Fry's verse in a landscape as incandescent as his words. The leaves on the nearby mountains were covered with gold-leafed aspens that tinkled and shimmered. The air was cool and brisk. Time fell away. I took long walks, bit into yellow apples, big and crisp, and felt I was crunching into fall itself. I was intoxicated with words.

I had no doubts about my genius. (I had my illusions as the loungers at Claude's had theirs.) There would be time enough to write my experiences. Meanwhile I would satisfy my appetites.

And I did. I lived for food and women. I wrote little and read carelessly. What interested me in poetry was sound, not meaning. Townsend marveled at my words, which was the reaction I craved. Or did Townsend truly marvel? Townsend, I learned months later, was a conman and liar, such a liar that he had perhaps convinced himself of the truth of his lies.

Later that fall, as Townsend repeated to me that he had been one of the three most promising young writers in America, he began reminiscing about his early years. He had been in the Korean conflict and told the story of a horrendous firefight he had experienced. As the shells pounded his platoon from all sides, Townsend saw his buddies screaming and calling for help as they were blown to bits. How he escaped was by the grace of God alone! As Townsend told this tale he began sobbing. He put his hand over his eyes. The sobs came louder; he cried and slunk off his chair onto the floor, kneeling and crying.

I tried to comfort Pete.

When I saw this performance a second time, I began to see Townsend as he was, but would not see a complete portrait until spring.

FIVE
Santa Fe (fall 1968)

During the fall, Hal's health continued to decline, though I was unaware of it. I still visited him, but now that I was teaching and socializing at Claude's I saw him less. One day word came to me that Hal was in the hospital. The next I heard, he had died.

The day of the service, a cold morning in December, I dressed and went to the church chapel. Hal's son, Jerry, stood outside the chapel doors and shook my hand, thanked me for coming and ushered me to a seat. Some people I recognized—Gene and Genie, Susie, Margaret and Leon, and a few others. Gene's head was bowed and his body aslant as he sat in a pew.

I sat stiff and uncomfortable. After the service ended I left at once; I had no desire to see anyone. I went instead to the memorial chapel where Hal's body lay. Two women stood before the casket. I looked at the body but did not recognize the face. Not recognizing the women either, I thought the man lying there was not Harold. This man's face and eyebrows were powder white. His cheekbones were prominent, his nose sharp and lips thin. This was a Spaniard, high bred but decadent, one who lived in the world of Catholic masses and arrogance. This man had been intolerant, with civilized manners that masked cruelty. As I left I saw one of the funeral home's employees and asked where Hal West lay and he pointed to the room I had just left.

Gene and Genie stood outside. They asked if I wanted to come with them, or go to Archie's for an Irish wake. I did not want to see Hal's body propped in a corner of the room and went instead with Gene and Genie and their eldest daughter, Diane, to Albuquerque.

***

At this moment I am thinking back on Hal and on Father, and in my mind they are sitting side-by-side.

Hal speaks, repeating what he said years before, "I'm sorry I taught you to drink."

No, you did not, Hal.

Father frowns.

Without my telling him, Hal knew there was an emptiness inside me, and why. One night as we stood at Hal's back door and he unlocked it, I said, "You're like a father to me."

"It's not the same, son," he said.

Surely he knew why I said that. That, I think, explains why he later told me, "Son, you'll succeed at whatever you want to do."

Father had never said anything like that, and I doubt he ever thought it.

Of the two men sitting side-by-side, the one I remember with great fondness is the one who opened the doors of America for me.

SIX
Santa Fe (fall 1968-summer 1969)

That fall I brought my new girlfriend, Paula, to Marlene's house. Paula was a bit plump but pretty, though not too bright. I brought her to Marlene's because I wanted to make an abrupt break with Marlene. After returning from New York and not having a steady girlfriend I would occasionally visit Marlene in the evenings. I thought if I lacked the will power to stay away, I could provoke Marlene into saying, "Don't come back!"

I called Marlene and asked if Alan and I could visit. Of course, she said. I did not tell Marlene about Paula, I simply brought her. Marlene seemed not to mind Paula's presence and offered us drinks as we sat in her living room. Paula and I sat side by side on Marlene's couch, while Alan sat on one chair and Marlene on another. After the first drink and much conversation about nothing, during which Paula must have wondered why I brought her to Marlene's, Marlene took Alan into her bedroom and left the door open. They stood next to her bed, talking. I was still watching them when Marlene shoved Alan onto the bed, landed on top of him and began kissing him ardently.

I knew why. Alan had told me earlier, in somewhat murky terms, that Marlene was giving him money for Gail and the boys, who now lived with Gail's mother. Since Alan wanted the money he chose to lie passively as Marlene attacked. While the attack proceeded, Paula and I left. My point had been made, and Marlene had made her counterpoint.

From that fall into winter I saw nothing of Marlene. By late fall I had seen the last of her, and never knew whether she remained in Santa Fe or moved elsewhere.

***

As fall progressed I was drawn further into Pete Townsend's world, enchanted by this romantic figure, clearly a talented man who had fallen into the depths. To a young person, especially perhaps to a young writer or artist there is something mesmerizing about the gifted man or woman whose talent has been ignored, or whose gifts have been squandered. Certainly for me there was. Pete Townsend threw me the bait, as he did to others, and I was hooked. Townsend piped a tragic tune full of alcoholic wisdom and for a time he became my Pied Piper, and for the next few months we met occasionally at Claude's to drink and play pool.

Later in the fall Townsend hooked up with Pamela Sanders, a lovely New Zealand émigré somewhere in her thirties with brown hair and blue eyes. Pamela owned a tea shop across the road from Hal West's former studio. The tea shop was one she had created out of a former home and had simple decorations painted on the walls and placed an assortment of tables and chairs throughout.

At the time Pete and Pamela hooked up, I thought nothing of their relationship; the different natures of this businesswoman and sophisticated alcoholic did not strike me. When Pete first moved in, he stopped going to Claude's. I would see Pete and Pamela together walking on Canyon Road and they seemed happy. A month later Pete was back at Claude's. For some reason it had not worked out between them and Pete was now renting an apartment on a side street off Canyon Road. One Friday afternoon after I returned from Espanola we collided at Claude's and began drinking. We drank bourbon all that afternoon and evening into the early morning when Claude's closed at 2:00 a.m. Afterwards I drove Pete to his apartment.

"Want to see what the dive looks like?"

"Sure."

Pete's small apartment was dark. Even with the overhead light switched on, the apartment was dark, with brown wood floors, tan paint on the walls, dark wood molding, a few pieces of wooden junk store furniture.

"How about a nightcap?" Pete asked.

He picked a pint of wine from the small kitchen table and extended it to me and I drank.

Outside a car passed and I thought about the drive home. I was tired.

"I'll see you tomorrow," I said.

The next day at mid-morning I was back at Pete's. "We need sustenance," Pete said. "Do you have some extra dollars? I'm tapped out."

"Sure," I said. We walked outside into the bright light, over to my car and got in. I drove us to a liquor store. This was new to me, this kind of drinking, but I was going to follow Pete, follow the high, follow Pete and the high and this new way of feeling.

Back in Pete's apartment we continued drinking until the wine was gone and we walked back outside. The sunshine felt good. I did not think of food, I was enjoying the high walking down the narrow curving street in the light and warm air. But the high faded by the time we bought a bottle of wine and walked back to Pete's.

Pete poured a drink for himself. "That's better." He held the bottle out.

I took it and poured a glass for myself.

"Anything to eat?"

Pete walked to the refrigerator and opened it.

"Bread."

"Got a toaster?"

"No."

I ate a slice of white bread and poured more wine into my glass. We drank and talked for hours.

The sky darkened, the apartment darkened, the sky blackened. I fell asleep in Pete's one padded chair.

I woke long after dawn with a bad taste in my mouth and a pounding head and a bad stomach. I closed my eyes, thinking sleep would end the pounding and the sickness. The bottle of wine and two empty glasses sat on the ugly wood kitchen table.

Pete walked slowly in.

"I'm fucked," he said. "Jesus, I'm fucked. Where's the wine?"

I held up the bottle. Pete took it and tilted it towards his glass.

"Shit," he said, "almost empty."

The wine had shut down my thoughts, my feelings. Except for one. I needed a drink. The world narrowed to the room, to me and Pete. I did not feel anything except the desire for a mouthful of wine. There in the dark room was this table, the bottle of wine.

Pete walked slowly to the table and picked up the bottle.
"Not much left," he said.

Pete could not hold his head up. When he did, I saw the bags under his eyes. He lowered himself to the floor and sat.

I got off my chair and moved to Pete, who held the bottle of wine. I tried to squat next to Pete to get hold of the bottle. I had to take my time trying to squat, I was shaking. I could not stop shaking. A tremor went through my arms and chest, then another. My arms, chest and legs shook faster. I hit the floor with my buttocks. Horrified I thought, "DT's. I've got the DT's!"

I could not drink any more. Shame slid over me. The shudders began again. The shuddering and the ache of the head would not stop.

In the spring Pete Townsend visited my casita, bringing his friend, Walter Gipp, a man whose name I had heard, one of those who drifted in and out of Santa Fe. Gipp's reputation was unsavory. He was said to have been the paid boyfriend of a Hollywood male celebrity.

I sat facing Gipp and Townsend as they sat on the couch. Gipp had the face of a man who not only lived inside a bottle but was depraved. The skin on his face was not pale but brownish and blotchy. His teeth were uneven and stained brown and he was nearly bald, with patchy hair sticking out behind his ears. Unlike Townsend, Gipp could not conceal his cunning. Townsend sat praising me, telling Gipp what a talent I was while Gipp nodded and looked approvingly and made comments meant to ingratiate himself.

Gipp was now living in Santa Fe and had found his old friend Pete Townsend and this old friend probably thought that one way of entertaining Walter was to see me.

***

On one afternoon months after I had last seen either of them, I walked into Claude's. Pete Townsend and Walter Gipp were standing at the bar. Townsend was wearing his brown sports coat. I had not seen him in months and the three of us chatted, and before I left I wrote a check for my beers.

About a week later, I began receiving returned check notices from my bank for amounts I did not recognize. Since I lived life by impulse, I did not always bring my checkbook and register with me. This day I had simply brought a block of checks. I went to the bank and was shown the checks written on my account. They were signed "Rob Wolf," in red ink. I realized that these checks had been written from the block I had brought to Claude's.

The bank reimbursed my account and the police were notified. I told my story to a police detective. The D.A. decided to prosecute Gipp, who probably had such a reputation in Santa Fe that even the police and district attorney knew of him.

A few months later the case went before a judge. Gipp now wore a sports jacket and assumed an expression of a complete innocence. He was represented by John Pruitt, a very confident lawyer in a searsucker suit who drilled the prosecution witnesses until we were not sure of our names. At one point Pruitt even had me wondering whether I had written those three bad checks. After the hearing, the cashier (who had cashed one of the forged checks), told me that she also had felt brutalized under Pruitt's cross-examination. But despite Pruitt's interrogations, Gipp was indicted. Neither the cashier, or I, or the investigating officer, had been given any preparation for a cross-examination.

The case did not go to trial for a year. By that time Pruitt had dumped Gipp, telling a partner in his firm that their office would not accept any more cases from people like Walter Gipp. Gipp's new lawyer had none of Pruitt's skill or fire and, expecting to have a humiliating experience before a jury, I was amazed at the mildness of his examination. The D.A.'s office was represented by the assistant D.A., a much more forceful man. At the pretrial meeting he instructed the investigating officer, the teller and me to begin our answers questions by saying, "To the best of my recollection." He also told a group of us, "The D.A. thinks it was Townsend, but we have Gipp, so we'll go after him."

I was certain that Gipp would be found guilty and was looking forward to hearing him receive a long, hard sentence.

I was not in the courtroom to hear the jury's verdict, but Gipp was found not guilty. The case hung upon the cashier's identification of Gipp as the person who presented the check at her window. The jury thought that since a year had passed since she last saw him, her identification was not reliable.

Gipp, I think, disappeared, but Townsend remained in Santa Fe and had not attended his friend's trial.

SEVEN
Chaquaco (1969)

In the winter of 1969 Gene and Genie decided to sell Chaquaco. They were in their fifties and young enough to remake their lives elsewhere. Their son Russell ranched in Wyoming and their eldest daughter, Diane, and her husband, Ed, had a ranch, somewhere also on the northern plains.

I visited Chaquaco occasionally on weekends, but also saw Gene and Genie in Santa Fe. One day they announced they had sold Chaquaco to a developer and would look for land in Wyoming. They asked if I would stay at the ranch while they were gone for two weeks, and feed the cattle and horses.

Since I was teaching in Espanola while I stayed at Chaquaco, I had to get up at five, dress and break the ice on the water tank for the horses and throw out feed. It was dark when I got up and walked to the kitchen and lit a kerosene lamp and made coffee.

The feeling of being miles away from anyone and alone on the plains was good. It felt especially good being at Chaquaco at night, when the feeling of aloneness was strongest.

In the early mornings I would eat, then walk out to the water tank—which would be frozen with a thin layer of ice—take a two-by-four and break the ice into pieces. I would take two or three hay bales out from the shed and break them open and lay them close by the tank. Then I would change into school clothes and drive fifty miles to Espanola.

In the afternoons I drove directly back from Espanola to Chaquaco, loaded Gene's pickup with hay bales and drove into the nearby pasture where the cattle were held. There was never much snow in winter in that part of New Mexico, and when it did snow the snow was usually gone the next day and someone feeding cattle never had to plow through snow drifts.

The one bit of excitement during those two weeks came the afternoon I found a young calf with its umbilical cord dried and tight around its middle. I did not want to cut and leave it dangling, so I drove five miles to Archie's camp. I had to drive: neither Archie nor Gene had telephones. Archie drove his pickup over and cut the cord with a penknife. "It's good you found her, Bob," he said. I was pleased to hear that, and pleased that I had saved a calf.

When Gene and Genie returned, they announced they had bought a ranch. The people I was closest to in Santa Fe were leaving. Was I going to stay in Santa Fe? Always New York City was buried somewhere in my mind. I would go there to live, eventually. I would have to, if I were to become the writer I wanted to be. Santa Fe in 1969 was a small city, almost a town, with a world famous opera and not much else in the way of culture. A writer who wanted to make his living in the theater could test a few pieces in Santa Fe, but could not remain there.

That spring Gene and Genie sold their cattle and moved north, and soon after school ended that spring, I went north to visit them, a brief two-week visit, before I drove to New York where I stayed with Larry Blake. Larry was now married, but his life was as crazy as ever as he struggled hopelessly with his drinking while trying and failing to renovate a Brooklyn three-story apartment house. Instead of looking for work in New York I played, and when the money ran out, I fled back to Santa Fe.

EIGHT
Santa Fe (fall 1970)

Sarah greeted me with a hug, saying, "I've missed you."

Sarah and I were friends from St. John's. She was a dark-haired, dark-complected beauty who supposedly had one of the largest divorce settlements for any woman in New Mexico. Sarah was sweet and generous but had no interests that I could see. I had been living with her before the New York trip, and now was back.

In the next few days I tried getting work with the New Mexico Public Schools, but I was hours short on meeting full certification. My emergency certificate had been good for two years only. When my money ran out, and nagged by Sarah's importunities, I went to the welfare office for food stamps. Since the food stamp recipient had to prove that he rented or owned a place, I bought a book of rent receipts and Sarah filled one out. I waited several hours in the welfare office sitting room, uneasy and embarrassed, before the receptionist called my name. I presented my rent receipt to the clerk and for fifty cents received $28.00 worth of food stamps.

Within a month my comfortable arrangement with Sarah collapsed and I went to my bank for a loan. With my Volkswagon as collateral, I secured a loan for $200 and found a studio apartment that rented for $65 a month. The apartment was one of a string of six ugly studios, dark and roach infested but furnished with a small table, a wooden chair and an oversized padded armchair.

I was driving throughout Santa Fe looking for "help wanted" signs. On the third day I spotted one in a shopping center. A large sign was displayed prominently in a window belonging to Skanks Drug Store. Skanks was announcing a grand opening.

Later, after thinking how humiliating it would be to work as a store clerk, I drove over.

The store was huge. The floor was tiled with brand new squeaking linoleum, while gleaming empty metal shelves stretched on and on.

About a dozen others, most younger than I, stood around the front of the store, filling out applications and eyeing one another.

On my application I wrote that I had a degree from Columbia University and had taught seventh grade math for two years. I handed the form to a young woman and sat down.

A minute later she called, "Wolf!"

Next to her was a tall, beefy man. She handed him my application.

He looked at it and said, "Hi, I'm John Stark. Come over here and have a seat."

Mr. Stark asked me why I had left teaching. I said it was not my cup of tea and was looking for something new. He said there was a lot of potential in working for Skanks. Skanks, he said, was a chain of stores and someone with ambition and drive could go places in it. I nodded and said I hoped so. He said I should return next Tuesday for another interview.

At the next interview Mr. Garcia, the store manager, was with Mr. Stark. Mr. Garcia was a dark, stout, little Mexican-American with a big voice. He asked me if I had ambition and I told him I did. He reiterated what Mr. Stark had said, that anyone who was determined to make something of himself could go far in the company. He himself, he said, had begun as a stock boy for Skanks in Las Cruces.

I did not care about becoming an assistant manager or a manager at Skanks. All I wanted was enough money to pay the rent and buy food and enough gas to drive to work and back until I could begin taking the courses at the College of Santa Fe that I needed for teacher certification.

"We're going to try you out as a stock boy," Mr. Garcia said. "You work hard, do a good job and we'll make it worth your while. For now you'll start at $2.25 an hour."

Two dollars and twenty-five cents an hour was ten cents an hour above minimum wage. But it was better than nothing, which was what I had. I was determined to work hard and get the raise Mr. Garcia made clear was the reward of a hard working Skanks employee.

The next morning I was given an ill-fitting red jacket and a nametag, which said, "Bob." I was led to a group of other new stock boys and stock girls.

We listened to a lecture from Mr. Stark, who explained that we were allowed twenty minutes for lunch and two ten-minute breaks, one in the morning and one in the afternoon. We were to be at work promptly. Three tardies and we were out, no excuses.

I felt like a jerk in my red jacket with a nametag. I dreaded the day that someone I knew would shop at Skanks. I told no one about my new career. Here I was, a graduate of an Ivy League university, about to cart dog food around a drug store.

We were each given a dolly and a razor blade and told to begin carting items out and stacking the shelves. I worked fast, efficiently cutting open the boxes with my razor blade, adjusting the numbers on the stamper, marking the prices and placing the cans onto shelves in neat, straight rows.

By the end of the second day we were ready for customers. A couple of heavily made up chicks ran the cosmetic counter. Garcia had definite ideas on what types of females could sell cosmetics. One was Mexican-American with eye shadow, mascara, rouge, red lipstick, long red nails, a bouffant hairdo, black net stockings, big tits, a tight dress and a beauty mark on one cheek. And a red Skanks jacket with a nametag. The other was her double, but Anglo and blonde. Garcia was hedging his bets.

Employees on my side of the store included a tall dark-haired female named Paula and a hefty Kiowa named Gil.

As stock boys and stock girls we were not supposed to talk with anyone besides customers. We only chatted among ourselves at breaks. When we socialized we stood around a hot water pot with instant coffee, sucking in cigarette smoke for ten minutes. If the women at cosmetics had ever passed through the stockroom when we were there, they would have said hello and no more. The women at cosmetics and liquors joked and laughed with the managers who joked and laughed back. We were, we realized, Skank's lowest caste.

After the first week I realized that at least two of the original workers on my side of the store were gone. I mentioned this to Gil and he said, yes, he had noticed it too.

My check was barely keeping me alive. I could not afford a phone or radio. I was so poor all I could afford to eat was a diet of pancakes and sausage for breakfast, a sandwich that I made for lunch, and hot dogs and beans for dinner. I could not afford good hot dogs, just the cheap ones that were dyed red and came in packages of thirty.

By the second week Mr. Stark approached me. "Bob," he said in his southern accent, "Mr. Garcia wants to see you upstairs."

I froze. What exactly had I done wrong?

"All right," I said, and followed Mr. Stark through the swinging doors and up the stairs to the office, which overlooked the store. Skanks had installed a large one-way window from which workers could be watched.

Mr. Garcia sat behind his desk.

"Have a seat, Wolf," he offered.

I sat down across the desk from him.

"We've been watching you," he began.

"He's gong to fire me," I thought.

"You're management material."

My eyes started.

"You're a good worker. You've done a good job, Wolf. This company rewards hard workers. Every manager in this company started out in the lower ranks, where you are. That's because it teaches them the nuts and bolts of the business."

He paused to look out the window. He pointed.

"There goes Eddie Rodriguez."

I saw a young kid in a red jacket walking towards our side of the store.

"Six months ago Eddie was a stock boy like you. Now he's an assistant manager. Eddie doesn't have a college education."

Garcia, I thought, probably did not have one either and was telling me what my Columbia University degree was worth.

"He's made it the hard way, with hard work. If you decide you want to succeed in life, you can do it with this company. Just keep working hard."

He smiled.

"It's a good company, Wolf," Mr. Stark added.

"All right?" Garcia said, ending the interview.

"Okay," I said.

"Now give it hell down there, buddy!" he shot at me.

"Right," I said.

I began thinking. I had no intention of staying, of course, but as long as I had to work there, why not be an assistant manager? I had completely forgotten that they already had two.

A few days later, as I was drinking coffee with Gil and Paula in the back room, Gil said, "Guess what?" There was a tone of assurance in his voice I had not heard before. "Garcia and Stark called me up for a talk the other day. They think I'm management material."

"They what?" Paula said. "They think you're management material? You? You've got to be kidding." Paula was not mean, but had a sarcastic sense of humor. Gil and I called her Acid Mouth.

"You're jealous 'cause you'd never make it in this company."

"Who would want to," Paula said.

"Gil," I said, "Sorry to destroy your illusions but they just told me that too."

"No!" Gil roared. "Those bastards!"

Paula laughed.

In the weeks that followed the three of us developed a bond: it was we against Skanks. Against Garcia, in particular. Stark, Gil informed us, was just a good-old Kentucky boy who had grown up poor and was happy to have his job. Gil and Stark had had a few beers together at the bowling alley across the street when Stark confided that.

About this time we began noticing that more and more of the faces we had seen with us at the store's opening were gone. We never heard about a firing; no one ever came into the stockroom downcast and said he had two weeks to find another job. We began to realize that Skanks did not give two-week notices. The Skanks' philosophy of management was simple: hold the carrot of promotion in front of employees and then fire a few at a time—steadily—to fill the rest with the fear. We knew what our eventual fate would be.

I began to hate the job. I was so grossly underpaid that when the head office in Salt Lake City made a mistake on my paycheck and shortchanged me, I had to borrow money from Mr. Stark. Garcia had flatly denied that the company had goofed. "This company doesn't make mistakes," he barked at me.

I accused the company of being a bunch of thieves.

"No one calls me a thief," Mr. Stark said and I nodded.

When repayment did come through, it was not for the full

amount and Garcia would not hear any more of it.

As Christmas approached, working at Skanks depressed me. Skanks represented everything that was vulgar in American life. Its merchandise was tawdry. Still, I used to gaze lovingly at the shelves of candy and carefully rearrange the boxes of games like *Monopoly* and *Spy* and *Tiny Tim's Game of Wonderful Things*, and wish that I could have the money to buy even one of them. I would occasionally open the Tiny Tim game to look at the cards and the board.

I was definitely outside the mainstream of American life, and Skanks began to represent the American machine. Men like Garcia were taking over the country. My response was to spend more time in the break room, and to steal candy from the back room. I would rip open a big chocolate bar, eat a hunk and hide the rest.

I began informing customers if items were defective. I also demonstrated items whenever a customer asked how something worked. That was good business, but I also knew that a good deal of Skanks' merchandise was, for one reason or another, defective. By demonstrating as many items as possible, I succeeded in killing numerous sales. Furthermore, if a customer seemed intent on buying an item which was chipped or cracked, but otherwise worked, I would tell him to demand a discount.

Eventually enough people were asking for discounts and demonstrations that Garcia called a staff meeting before work one day and told us in no uncertain terms that we were not to demonstrate goods or advise people to ask for discounts. I was sure he had seen me demonstrating items. Did he know I was suggesting discounts?

Gil and Paula were as bitter as I. They, too, were taking long coffee breaks and taking more time loading their dollies, stamping cans and boxes, and shelving them. They were spending more time talking with customers. The three of us were going out for beers after work. We talked about what we would do.

I said I would return to teaching, but I would have to take additional math and education courses to obtain a teaching certificate. Paula also said she would return to school for psychology.

Gil wanted to do theater.

Then it happened. One day Gil came into the back room as Paula and I were drinking coffee. He told us bitterly that he had been fired and had to leave at once. A week later Paula was canned.

Shortly after Paula left, I was accepted by the College of Santa Fe. I needed Skanks' paychecks until classes began in January, but one day, as I dawdled at hauling the trolley, Stark came by and said that Mr. Garcia wanted to see me at once.

Garcia was seated behind his desk scribbling on forms and looked up when I came in behind Stark. He threw his pencil on the desk.

"Wolf," he said, "when you came here I thought you were a hard worker. You've disappointed us. You don't care about your work and you don't do much of it. I'm firing you. You'll be sent a check in the mail that'll pay you up till today."

I nodded. I now had joined Gil and Paula. We still hung out, and we learned six months later that Garcia and Eddie Rodriguez had both been fired. It was obvious why Garcia had been fired, but we were not so sure about Eddie. Stark soon afterwards got disgusted with the company and returned to Kentucky.

NINE
Santa Fe Mid-High School (1971-74)

On an early afternoon I was standing at the La Fonda bar talking with the Hispanic man next to me. He had come with two friends, probably businessmen or state employees, all dressed in sports jackets and ties.

In those days Hispanics still came to the cantina in La Fonda. There was a nice, easy back and forth between the races, not like today, when they seldom mingle.

We must have talked for a while before I told the man that I had taught in Espanola. "I taught two years on an emergency certificate. Last month I completed teacher certification. There's a math opening at Mid-High, but Phil Martinez wouldn't speak with me."

Phil Martinez was the principal at Mid-High.

"George Hacker is a friend of mine," the man said. "He owes me a favor. I'll speak to him."

George Hacker was superintendent of Santa Fe Public Schools.

The next day I received a call from Phil Martinez, apologizing for his abruptness and asking if I could meet him at his home. I drove to his house and we sat in chairs on his front porch where he repeated his apology and offered me the job.

"You can't be late. No more tardies."

He had obviously heard about how often I had been tardy while student teaching. I started to protest my innocence and he cut me off with, "Don't be tardy."

In those days Santa Fe was a very small city, more like a town. Who you knew meant much, and so did face-to-face encounters.

I had completed my certification with courses in math, teaching methods, and psychology. One of our assigned readings, *Summerhill*, had an unfortunate influence on my classroom control, or lack of it. Summerhill was the name of a tiny English boarding school, a haven for children with learning disabilities and behavioral problems. Children could attend classes if they wished, and break windows if they wished. The child was allowed to act out all impulses. Summerhill's founder, A.S. Neil, believed that once a troubled youngster acted out his anger, he would eventually become a normally socialized youngster. As I did not want to be authoritarian, this philosophy appealed to me.

My psychology professors at the College of Santa Fe were sympathetic to this view. Consequently during my first year at Mid-High I tolerated chaos. Students would talk and laugh with each other whenever they pleased, practically bounce off the walls, and I would tell myself I was not distressed. The second semester I tried clamping down, without success. Experienced teachers later told me not to crack a smile from the beginning of fall semester until Thanksgiving.

The next year I followed that advice. Teaching became fun,

in large part because of a book, *How to Survive in your Native Land*, by James Herndon. *How to Survive in Your Native Land* was both a series of comic narratives of Herndon's teaching experiments and an exploration of America. In a series of interpretive essays, Herndon explained why the public school system, and it is a system, reflected much that had gone wrong with America. Anyone who thought much about the relation between the two realized that the public school system was the product of the mechanical mode of thinking.

For example, everything in the school day is prescribed, marked and demarcated: the day is divided into periods of equal length: one moves at the sound of a bell to the next room: announcements are piped over a loud speaker: buses deliver students to school and from school: students sit in rows: they listen to lectures: they take tests: tests divide them into winners and losers.

Students do not want to be there. But what choice do they have?

Herndon likened most public school lessons to lectures on Egypt—irrelevant to anything outside the classroom, while the classroom environment was antithetic to real learning.

While I understood all that Herndon was saying, I was still enthusiastic about teaching. Like Herndon, I wanted to make a difference in my students' lives. Somehow. The classroom became fun.

How to Survive in Your Native Land came at a time when California was having an influence on the national culture. Herndon was a California product and *How to Survive in Your Native Land* projected the low-key California life that seemed a perpetual summer of baseball fields, trout fishing, and afternoon beers with friends. I do not know if anyone else at Mid-High read this book, but many of us acted as if we had. We in our group loved teaching and went out for beers together on Friday afternoons.

One of my classes the first year was filled with bright, attentive students. We liked being together and about a dozen joined me once a week after school for improvisational acting exercises. How different from my two years in Espanola!

I had answered Herndon's question, "How do we survive in

our native land"? His answer was, "By finding our work." I had found mine, just as he had found his—in teaching.

TEN
(Santa Fe)

Tony Padilla, one of the teachers at Mid-High, has been a friend to this day. Tony is descended from one of the earliest colonists in northern New Mexico. This forebear was given a large tract of land that covered much of present day Santa Fe. Tony is proud of this forebear and of his own Hispanic heritage. But Tony, who grew up in a barrio and as a youngster spoke only Spanish, watched the traditions of northern New Mexico disappear amid the enveloping Anglo culture.

For the years when Tony was a boy in Santa Fe, Hispanic heritage was strong. It was Catholic. Many of Tony's people heated with wood, made their own tortillas, cooked pots of beans, and spoke Spanish to one another. Tony, as a man, did the same.

In the days when Tony graduated from high school, there were few jobs for young men in Santa Fe. Tony joined the army, spent time in Texas, Michigan, and Germany, but saw nothing that he cared for more than New Mexico, and when he was discharged, returned to Santa Fe.

But as Tony saw Hispanic heritage weakening, he worked consciously to keep it alive in himself. He heats his home with wood, and in the fall used to drive his pickup into the mountains to cut wood with a friend. The two took turns cutting the piñon and juniper with a chainsaw and stacking it in the pickup. Every fall they drove into the mountains and cut enough wood for both of their families for winter heat. Sometimes Tony's wife made the trip with him and the two of them cut and stacked wood.

Tony made one trip by himself into the mountains and was cutting a log when the chainsaw jerked out of the log and into his leg, cutting a huge flap of flesh. Tony turned off the chainsaw, put it in the back of the pickup and made a tourniquet around his leg, which was bleeding badly. It bled badly all the way back to Santa

Fe and the hospital emergency room.

Tony held onto his heritage in other ways. Fishing and hunting were two of the ways. Once Tony invited me to a dinner at his grandmother's house, where he prepared rabbits he had just shot; I almost broke a tooth before picking buckshot out of my mouth.

Tony's parents did not have the money to raise all of their children and gave Tony, their youngest, to his grandmother, who lived in a barrio. Tony's young friends spoke Spanish among themselves. Tony's grandmother spoke English but not to him. Tony, who spoke only Spanish, was completely bewildered and shamed his first day in school and did not want to return. That night and for many nights thereafter, Tony's grandmother sat him down and taught him English.

Later she taught him to cook northern New Mexico foods, and once he was married Tony cooked their evening meals. By cooking northern New Mexico food, cutting wood and heating with wood, hunting and fishing, Tony was keeping hold of himself. After all, what did the Anglos have? What traditions from Europe did Anglos maintain? Their technologies superseded one anther so rapidly they had no culture to hold onto. Even their beliefs had died too.

Indigenous peoples and Hispanics had a chance of staying awake so long as they did not mindlessly adopt all that American culture offered them. What modern American culture did offer were narcotics of various kinds: cars, phones, garbage disposals, electricity, toasters, television sets . . . More and more people forgot how to do for themselves and fell asleep.

By the time I met Tony, he was married to his second wife, Donna, an Anglo woman from southern New Mexico, where the Anglos do not like "Mexicans." Donna's family did not like Donna marrying a "Mexican."

In the days when Tony and I taught together, one of our hangouts was the Plaza Bar. The Plaza was a magnet for all sorts, from newspaper editors and former television actors to Indian artists and battling women.

Tony and Donna told of the afternoon they were at the Plaza, listening to Gilbert Gonzales, a friend of Tony's, go on and on about how everyone today was a conformist and robot. "We're all programmed," Gilbert claimed. "We're all robots."

Tony objected. "I'm not. I make a point of not being one. I do things."

Gilbert would not let it drop. "We're all robots."

Tony said, "If you feel that way, let's do something far out, something crazy."

"Like what?"

"Let's take off our clothes and run up Washington Avenue."

Washington Avenue is one of Santa Fe's main downtown streets, running three blocks from the Plaza past the police station to the Masonic temple.

Gilbert would not do it.

Tony said, "You watch me."

Gilbert would not even watch him; that was too far out.

Tony and Donna walked to their Volkswagen where Tony took off his clothes except for his socks and shoes. Donna drove him to the end of Washington Avenue at the Plaza where Tony got out and began running. He ran a block past the library, past the police station, and up another block to the Masonic temple, where Donna waited with their car.

That was Santa Fe then, and that was Tony Padilla, a singular man.

Fifty years after Tony made his naked run in downtown Santa Fe, Hispanic culture has mostly disappeared from Santa Fe. A growing number of young people, I am told by older Hispanics, cannot speak Spanish. Many cannot find jobs. Maybe they take drugs and the girls get pregnant—the old story.

Tony is now in his late seventies and has had many accidents. He applies a marijuana ointment to his knee to try and kill the pain, but it is a temporary fix. Still, he cooks for his wife, who is now frail and ill, but Tony can no longer go into the mountains to cut wood. The reminder of former days in the mountains preparing for winter is stacked along their side fence—a long, tall stack of piñon and juniper.

ELEVEN
Santa Fe (spring 1971)

When I saw Pete Townsend next, his face had sagged further and he had none of the old braggadocio. He had, however, discovered a widow, a nice woman who liked to drink and believed the stories Pete told her. It seemed that she had enough money to take care of them both. Pete made a point of looking me up, after almost a year, to introduce me to his wife. He brought her around to his other friends, the few that he had.

Jim Wing was one of his few friends. Jim had known Pete for several years. They had probably met at Hal West's studio. Jim was probably in his late fifties and lived on a quiet, dead end side street off Canyon Road where he had built his own adobe house and surrounded it with a wild garden filled with small Russian olives and raised beds of flowers and grasses. Jim had also carved a half dozen totems on flat boards with his own idiosyncratic designs and placed them around the garden. A pueblo Indian friend visited Jim and asked the meanings of the totems, and Jim said they meant nothing, which proved to the Indian that they indeed had secret meanings.

After Hal's death I began to see more of Jim. Being with Jim gave me the same sense of peace and connectedness that I had at Hal's. Jim had been a painter but years later began writing novels. Pete had recommended Jim and his novels to his agent, Mary Bradley, and she had signed Jim. But Mary did no more for Jim than she did for Pete, or for me, many years later, long after Pete died.

Pete sincerely admired Jim's novels, which frequently used dreams and inserted surreal events into the everyday. Peculiar things could happen in Jim's novels. There was, for one, the man who fell out of the sky, pinwheeling with arms and legs outstretched, landing like a bug on a bus windshield. Other novels were skewed only slightly, which added whimsical touches to the everyday. None were ever published.

Jim was fairly reclusive. He left his adobe house off a quiet backstreet only to go for his daily constitutional walks, or to shop.

Jim did not go to bars or theaters for plays or movies. He had a telephone but rarely answered it. The only times Jim and Pete met were when Pete visited Jim.

Pete brought his wife to visit Jim, and like me, Jim thought the woman was nice, but said, "She believes everything he tells her." We both felt sorry for the woman, and when Pete died a year later Pete's widow sent Jim a letter about Pete's last year and how much he liked Jim. Jim later wrote a novel about Pete Townsend, which began with a larger-than-life-sized statue of Pete Townsend, an American war hero, being erected in a public square.

But while he was married, and a year before he died, Pete often arrived at Jim's house and helped himself so lavishly to the vodka that Jim always kept under the kitchen sink, and was such a bore and visited so often that Jim wanted to stop him coming. Jim took a black marker, and on a piece of cardboard wrote, "Sick and can't be bothered this means you" and wedged it on the inside of his front screen door.

I saw it several times and did not bother to knock but walked away. The third time I saw it I knocked and kept calling, "Jim! Jim!" Jim was not only somewhat of a recluse but also hard of hearing. Finally he came to the door.

"I saw this sign, Jim, and I didn't know whether to knock or not."

"Oh, that's not for you, Bob. You're welcome anytime. That's for Pete Townsend."

Somehow Pete discovered that someone had visited Jim despite the sign and the next time he saw Jim he wanted to know why Jim had let this person in.

"Oh, that was Harvey," Jim told him. "He's a hippie. He doesn't believe in signs."

The death of Pete Townsend was like a period—an end-stop—to a segment of my life. The center of my socializing had already shifted from Claude's to a group of young artists who met twice weekly in Saul Gaster's tower studio, but Pete's death symbolized a severance with the darker elements on Canyon Road.

TWELVE
The Four Corners (1972-73)

From at least the time of D.H. Lawrence and Mabel Dodge, disaffected urbanites have found refuge in the primitive sanctuary of New Mexico. It is a stark land, best appreciated after driving, say, through Oklahoma and the Texas Panhandle. Eastern Oklahoma is almost Midwest—some parts green and rolling. But western Oklahoma with its flat land and sparse grass, mesquite and sage belongs to the Great Plains. The Texas Panhandle is more primitive, less cut to human scale or aspirations. Then comes New Mexico. Fifteen miles across the Texas border suddenly there are mesas, uprises of land flattened on top, dotting an almost empty landscape. The land seems flatter, longer, more primitive.

The ancient cultures here once seemed primitive, even at the turn of the last century when Lawrence and his friends, filled with the words of an exhausted civilization, arrived and found themselves renewed by the Other. One used to see the Otherness expressed in New Mexico mountain towns built of baked mud houses pitched on the sides of hills with their twisted, rutted streets. The people used to stare at you. And in their churches, the crucified Christs, not serene in death but tortured, gape in agony. I had seen the same Otherness in photographs in Penitente rites and processions in those villages, and in a small one-room Penitente building, a morada, into which I and a few others had been allowed to visit. Here was a room set aside for meditation and prayer once a year, during Easter week. No one knows how many males in each mountain village now belong to the Penitente Brotherhood. The Penitente rites in each town last from Lent through Easter Sunday. At night on Good Friday, the darkest day of the Christian calendar, the Brothers used to proceed through their towns, shaking chains and chanting ancient modal hymns. They would flagellate themselves in a rite of purification. In former times the Penitentes crucified a man during Easter week. It was an honor to be chosen. If the crucified one died, his shoes were placed on the doorstep of his home.

I had experienced the Other outside one of the seven Hopi

Pueblos. Each of the seven pueblos was built atop a different mesa. I had driven to one of the mesas from Santa Fe all night to attend a dance the next day. I arrived before dawn, and at the base of a mesa, driving with windows down, I heard drumming. I drove to the base of the mesa, parked and climbed upwards. As I approached the ridge of the mesa and the drumming got louder, the sun rose, a great yellow half circle, its base the mesa itself, and into that half-circle stepped a man in buffalo headdress, singing, chanting, holding out a buffalo robe. I stood transfixed, hurled back untold years into that which lies beyond words.

It ended. I stepped behind a rock, but they had seen me, and another man, dressed in deer antlers and shaking rattles, came to exorcise my presence. I left.

I came to New Mexico, not to be immersed in the Other, but to find a culture and people that had not been standardized. For that reason people still come to Santa Fe, even though it is now changed into a stage set of its former self and the newcomers, ironically, are themselves standardized.

I had dreamed of going west for years, and finally in my eighteenth summer I took off, hitchhiking to San Francisco by way of New Mexico and Arizona. That is how one of my drivers and I came upon Duran.

Looking for that which is authentic is one reason why during summers I drove my black Volkswagen beetle into desert country, into Arizona and through Monument Valley into Utah. I would head west on Route 66 to Gallup, a town at the western edge of New Mexico. Gallup is a railroad town on the edge of the reservation with a lot of bars and tourist shops selling Navajo and Zuni jewelry. It is a town with Indians on the streets and in the shops and bars.

West of Gallup you enter the Navajo reservation, a dry, sandy land of sparse grass, buttes and rocks. Further west and north lays the vast Monument Valley, whose rock spires and buttes comprise a prehistoric, sacred landscape.

On my first trip to the valley I headed for Goulding's Trading Post, which in those days was one of the few marks on a map of the valley. The trading post was a red stone building built in

1921 for trade with the Navajos. In the Depression, Mr. Gouldiing saved his business by bringing photographs of Monument Valley to John Ford. Goulding's son, I think it was, stood next to me and pointed to the land below and said that was where Ford's crews pitched tents. There had been camaraderie in those days between crew and actors, before the days when stars had their own trailers. The man pointed to the dirt road running into the valley and said that is where the stagecoach in the film "Stagecoach," was chased by Indians.

On my last trip through Monument Valley, on my way to the Goosenecks in Utah, I passed two posts with a cross beam on top that I recognized from a western film. A character had been hanged from the crossbeam. I pulled the car over and walked across the road to see the structure. I thought it strange that it was still there, years later. I heard a rifle shot from behind and stopped. Someone had fired a shot at me from the massive rock formations in back. I was sure that was not meant to hit but to warn me off Navajo land. I walked back to my car, imagining myself in rifle crosshairs. Whoever fired that shot did not shoot again.

From there I drove north through the valley into Utah, a land also belonging to the Other. I had no plan, I just drove. I crossed the wide San Juan River and followed signs to the Goosenecks. A road led me up onto rock a thousand feet above the San Juan River. Below, the river twisted in snakelike coils, and has twisted for 300 million years, and in its flowing has cut giant ziggurats—stepped pyramids—from the rock.

That on which I stood was rock, a giant bread loaf. The thousand foot cliffs that lined the winding San Juan were composed of giant rocks, all shaped like loaves of bread, one stacked atop another, with a depression where the edges of four bread loaves met.

The sun beat on the rock, heating it and reflecting up. Forty miles distant, hazy, were the rock formations of Monument Valley. On the horizon, thunderheads moved towards the Goosenecks. The sun was blocked, the sky darkened and rain fell fast, and passed over. I looked in the hollows where the loaves met and saw tiny crustaceans wriggling about. Whatever these were, they were able to dry and remain dormant once the water evaporated.

I drove on, up into desert hill country where I came upon a deserted mining town of grayed and weathered shacks. In front of one shack near the road a sign proclaimed that Zane Gray had lived there. For years I thought of returning to that shack and staying a day or two, or a week, and writing.

***

In those years when I spent part of each summer driving through desert country, I also spent weekend evenings in Santa Fe at Claude's, which was where I met Billy Herrera. Billy was a pueblo Indian with a deep chest and ponytail. Through Billy I got to know his friend, Paul, a Commanche.

One summer afternoon Billy, Paul, and I rode in Billy's old Ford down to Hardy's bar and trading post, which was several miles from Cochiti Pueblo. Billy was from Cochiti, Paul was Comanche, and I was a white man interested in Indian ways, and just glad to be with friends. Billy was just the type for me to know. Only two months earlier he had been arrested by tribal police for being drunk in the pueblo and held in jail until one of his family could pawn Billy's rifle at Hardy's for enough money to make bail. That was why we were driving down to Hardy's, for Billy to pay some more on the pawn.

After Billy made a payment we shuffled around the old shop with sagging wood floors, looking at the rifles and fishing rods and the cases of silver and turquoise jewelry before going into the bar and ordering beers. I went to the jukebox and shoved in three quarters.

A man named Jordy was tending bar. I asked him if he knew Gene West.

"I'm not sure," he said.

"He's a tall fella worked on Cochiti dam."

"Oh, yeah. No, I ain't seen him lately."

"He's moved to Wyoming."

The bar in Peña Blanca was one of my favorites. I said to Billy and Paul, "Let's go to Peña Blanca. There's a good bar there."

"Let's do it," Paul said and we ambled back to the truck.

Billy said, "Cochiti first."

We headed off on a dirt road.

Billy was still amiable, enjoying the country the same as Paul and me. Billy and I were feeling good, but Paul was sober. Once we drove into the pueblo, Billy started knocking my whiteness and putting me down for not being Indian. It kept getting worse.

When we braked in front of Billy's house, Billy went in, and Paul said, "Man, he's riding you."

"Yeah, but fuggit."

"It irritates you."

"Yeah."

"I told him not to ride you so hard. Back when you got out to take a piss, I says to Billy, 'You're ridin' him. Ease up. He doesn't know any of this Indian stuff. Give him time to learn.' He says, 'Was I giving him a hard time?' I says, 'You sure were.' 'Alright, I'll ease up.'

"Like now, Bob, he's even putting me down. He didn't ask us to go in with him. He always used to ask me. But when he gets this way, before he gets drunk, when he knows he's gonna really get drunk, he'll ask me to drive. If he doesn't, then I say, 'Billy, you better let me drive.' If he says no I press him until he gives me the keys. I can always get them. Billy acts strong, like now, but he really wants someone to tell him what to do."

Once Billy returned and we drove to Peña Blanca, Billy said, "The family I visited at Cochiti, the old man had a bridle stolen from him and he's out on horseback looking for the man that stole it. Police are after him too."

At Peña Blanca we parked in the dirt yard beside the old bar with grey-stuccoed walls. Beside the bar an old man sat on horseback under a towering cottonwood. I did not need Billy to tell me that that this was the old man looking for his bridle and the man who stole it. An old car also sat under the cottonwood. Sitting on this car covered with bird shit was a young man. Billy and the old man and the boy greeted each other in Tewa. In English, Billy introduced Paul and me to the old man and the boy.

The old man held a pint of wine and the boy sat with a quart of beer. We needed more beer. Paul and I gave fifty cents each to Billy and Billy went into the bar to buy two quarts.

A few minutes later we were all comfortably drinking. The boy and I sat on the car hood, Billy and Paul on fenders, and the old man on horseback. Suddenly we heard shouting from across the road. Out of the weeds, coming up out of the bank appeared a stout Indian wearing a t-shirt and Levi's rolled up to his knees, jerking one knee high in the air, then another, moving towards us, carrying a pint of wine and cussing. He was clowning for us.

The old man, the boy and Billy began laughing and jeering. It was not mean but tongue-in-cheek, Indian mocking.

"Hector!" they shouted.

Hector, grinning, plopped himself down alongside the tree, next to us.

"Hey, Koshare!" the other Indians shouted.

The Koshare are masked and painted clowns that dance at spring fertility rites.

"You wanted to be a medicine man but they wouldn't let you," the old Indian jeered.

Hector made a face.

The others laughed.

One elbow bracing him as he lay on the ground, Hector said, "Goddammit. I'm walking down the acequia, down at Tapia's and he asks if I want to work. 'Sure,' I say, and we work down there in this hot and he send me here for wine."

Old Mr. Tapia, I thought, will never see his sixty cents or dollar again.

Billy stood, lifted the quart bottle and flung it across the field. He stood at the edge of the acequia and started towards it. He slid, then pitched onto the ground. He squawked and began crying. He sat up slowly.

"What's the matter, Billy?" Paul asked.

Billy let out a long wail. "My shoulder!"

"He's dislocated his shoulder," Paul said. "Billy . . . let's fix it."

Hector took hold of Billy's wrist while Paul held Billy. Hector pulled, Billy screamed.

Hector took a small sack from his belt and began singing in Tewa and sprinkling corn in the four directions.

A month later, sitting at Claude's, I showed Billy the story I had written about the healing and he tore it up. "That was not for writing. I wanted you to see something of the Indian way."

***

Another day after several beers the three of us visited the Santa Fe Indian School. We stood in a kitchen of one of the school buildings. Billy and Paul were standing next to a drawer of utensils. They began arguing, shouting. Billy shoved Paul, who staggered backwards, opened a draw and grabbed a large knife. He slashed at Billy, who screamed and fell.

His hair hanging over his face and swaying slightly, Paul stared at me and demanded, "Do you want some of the same, white man?"

I could not speak.

"Do you?"

Billy stood and they both laughed.

"Were you worried, Bob?" Paul asked.

"Hell, yes."

"Billy and I did stunt fighting for tourists." Paul named a faux western town built for a tourist attraction.

That fight was another piece of Indian humor.

***

One or two summers later I headed once more for Monument Valley, but left Santa Fe late afternoon. I decided to reach the valley by reservation dirt roads. I had a state map that showed one such road running through the reservation to the valley. What it did not show, naturally, were all the smaller dirt roads running off of it. I arrived at the Navajo reservation long after dark. The moon was no more than a sliver of light, and all I could see was what my headlights illuminated, a narrow cone.

I found my road and followed it for miles before I came to a Y. I paused, then picked one of the roads at random and continued.

I came upon another dirt road, then another. Each time I picked turns at random. Then I was suddenly at someone's camp, with a home of some sort. I could not see it clearly. I braked. Dogs jumped into the headlights and barked. I turned my wheel left, threw the car into reverse and heard one of the dogs howl in pain. The dwelling stayed dark. I felt sick at the sound and at what I had done, but I put the car into drive and sped away, with the dog still howling.

THIRTEEN
Santa Fe 1973-1974

I met Elizabeth in Santa Fe while she was acting in one of my plays. That was the winter of 1973. We married in the spring. A week after the wedding Elizabeth took her two-week vacation. We had decided to spend it hitchhiking to the Grand Canyon and back. We did not carry sleeping bags, but stuffed our knapsacks with clothes. This was a honeymoon that suited both of us.

A friend drove us to the edge of Santa Fe and from there two rides took us south to Clines Corners, a huge gas station and tourist shop on Route 66. The next ride took us through Albuquerque, and from there we traveled through desert country, through half a dozen towns, past isolated curio shops and gas stations painted bright colors.

One ride left us off in the middle of Gallup, New Mexico, a hard town close to the Arizona line, near the Zuni and Navajo reservations. We walked west through Gallup, past more curio shops, bars, and Indians. The town was filled with Indians who had hit the edge of nowhere. We stopped for soda pops and stood watching the scene.

We waited an hour outside Gallup before getting a ride to Flagstaff. It was dusk when we found a motel. The next morning we began hitching north to the Grand Canyon.

Photographs cannot prepare us for the immensity of the canyon that has been cut over aeons by fast flowing water. Pondering the patience and strength of the water, the immensity of the cut and its indifference to our existence is to awaken to the incongruence between organic life and this immeasurable inanimate process. Here human life truly seems an accident and alien presence. I came to the Grand Canyon intending to hike Bright Angel Trail, which leads from the canyon's south rim down to the Colorado River. Since the early 20th century, guides have led tourists on mules up and down Bright Angel. From the rim one sees the trail switching back and forth, winding its way down to the river, through millions of years of stratified red, black, and brown rock.

While Elizabeth stayed on the south rim, I made the eight-mile trek down and up the narrow dirt trail, dotted with hikers, pausing at least once against the side of the cliff to let a mule train pass.

The next afternoon we began hitching back to Santa Fe. Our second ride came from two women in a pickup. When they pulled over, we ran for it. The driver was a Navaho woman in her thirties; her mother sat next to her. The mother rolled down her window and the driver leaned forward and told us to get on the truck bed, where they had baskets of laundry. We climbed over the tailgate and sat on our packs. When they stopped to wash their clothes at a Laundromat, we sat inside with them. Both women wore skirts and blouses and wore their black hair cut short below their ears.

The daughter's name was Delphine. She asked where we were from and why we were hitching. When their clothes had dried and we went back outside, Delphine said, "Sit inside with us" and the four of us crowded inside the cab. Elizabeth sat on my lap.

After more talk Delphine asked if we had ever been to a squaw dance.

"No."

"We are having one tonight. Would you like to come?"

"Yes," we told her.

Delphine drove off the pavement onto a dirt road. Miles later we came to a camp, filled with a large gathering of Navajos, the women in billowy bright colored skirts and blouses and the men wearing jeans and flat, wide-brimmed hats or a cloth tied around the brow and knotted to the side. Pots hung over fires. A line of sheep's' heads lay in a row nearby. Pickup trucks were scattered across the encampment of men, horses and hogans.

By now it was dusk and Elizabeth wandered off. Delphine must have looked over at me and saw that Elizabeth was gone and said, "Don't let her be by herself. She'll get raped."

I walked through the encampment until I found Elizabeth. "Don't wander off," I said. "Delphine said it's not safe."

Delphine had earlier told us, "Tonight and tomorrow morning our clan hosts a healing ceremony for another clan. Tomorrow after sunup they leave and we go to their camp and they sing for us."

At dark we watched the dancing and listened to the drumming and singing and thought to ourselves we were hungry. A moment later Delphine came and asked if we would like food. She led us to the fire where we got plates and filled them with fry bread, pinto beans and mutton. We squatted on the ground and ate.

Later, when the singing was over, Delphine said we would sleep on the flatbed of her truck and brought us blankets. She and her family slept out of doors, under a tarp set on four tree limbs set as posts next to their hogan. We lay down and covered ourselves with the blankets and tried to sleep but the metal flatbed was cold. Even curling together we were cold. Delphine returned, saying, "If you're cold, sleep in the hogan."

We carried the blankets inside the hogan, which was warm and neat, with a few pieces of furniture and woven blankets of warm color. We slept on a bed.

Our hosts, hardened to life, had no problem sleeping out of doors, perhaps under a pile of sheepskins and blankets.

The next morning we stood with her family in a large group alongside another hogan. At the front of this hogan stood an oval of people—the visiting clan—twenty feet from the door. Suddenly objects began flying out of the door and high into the air—a rifle, a bolt of cloth, a hat—a multitude of things useful. Now I understood a painting I had given Gene West years before. The same scene had been depicted in gouache by Navajo artist, Andy Tsihnahjinnie. Delphine and her mother stood next to us. "We are giving our guests presents," she told us. "Tomorrow we will spend the night at their camp and the next morning they will give us gifts."

After the guests decamped and returned to their village to ready that night's feast, Delphine drove us to the highway and we exchanged addresses. A month later we received a letter from her, saying that she wanted to make rings for us. What symbols did we want on them? Elizabeth and I talked briefly and could decide nothing. I wrote back saying, "Whatever symbol you want." That was the last we heard from Delphine. Not understanding the importance of symbolism, being whites in a culture that had abandoned symbolism centuries earlier, we could not grasp what our response might mean to her.

Elizabeth and I remained in Santa Fe for a year after our marriage. In June 1974 we resigned our jobs and prepared to move to Douglas, Michigan, a small town a few hours' drive north of Chicago.

Our friends in Santa Fe were few. Alan Hays and Gail had divorced and Alan was engaged to a younger woman and about to vacation with his fiancée in Mexico. Jim Wing was well and still writing. Besides Alan and Jim, I saw few of my old friends except Tony and Donna Padilla.

One of our friends held a party shortly before we left. Alan Hayes was there. We made vague plans to meet in the future when we would study together, teach each other and develop intellectually. To my regret, we never corresponded. I lost track of Alan until the St. John's alumni directory listed him as living Paris.

FOURTEEN
Then and Now

In the years when I first roamed America, I had no fears for myself. I was young. For the first fifteen years of wandering I never encountered antagonisms, or threats, or danger. The people who helped me, and they were many, were genuinely solicitous for my well-being—even the bums on the Phoenix Skid Row.

But I was far from the only young male wandering the country. Many others were hitchhiking across America. For each of us this was an exploration, a discovery of others and of ourselves, an unknowing test of our abilities and limits.

There existed in America in the early sixties a wonderful energy. John Kennedy, a young man coming to office after the elderly Eisenhower, exuded optimism. His assassination checked it, but Lyndon Johnson's War on Poverty and Civil Rights legislation gave us new hope. In a 1964 commencement address at Howard University, Johnson said, "Freedom is the right to share, share fully and equally in American society—to vote, to hold a job, to enter a public place, to go to school."

In the early sixties I wrote a long paragraph meant to be the introduction to a book on America. The paragraph consisted of a string of iconic American images—places and things I had seen. It ended by calling America "a giant of the morning."

So I believed it to be.

I believed then, as possibly others believed, that America was just coming into power, that it was like a young man stretching and readying himself for another day. The land was hopeful.

I was sure that the people of New Canaan were an aberration, that most Americans—tradesmen, and farmers, and ranchers, the working people of America—were good-natured. The broad smile and strong handclasp was for me a symbol of the comradeship I felt existed in small towns, on farms and ranches, characteristic of the essential American character. I had not read Whitman, but I too envisioned a land of comrades.

I was young.

When one friend read what I wrote about hitchhiking and riding freights in the early sixties, he said, "You had a lot of guts."

No, I did not. Not fearing is not the same as having courage. One has courage when one experiences fear but perseveres on a course despite it. I was impelled and excited to see Americans and the American landscape.

Another friend wrote that I was trusting. Yes, I was. I had no reason not to be. I had lived my life in safe communities, never confronted by aggressive or threatening adults. Besides, the news in those years did not focus on murders, fraud, kidnappings, bombings and mass killings. We white middle-class Americans had not yet learned to fear our neighbors.

* * *

Even into the early 1980s life on the road was relatively safe. With one exception I was treated with the same kindness and generosity that I experienced in the early sixties. The exception came in 1982, hitchhiking from Vaughan, New Mexico to nearby Duran. Before leaving Santa Fe for Vaughan, I heard from friends that bodies had been discovered alongside New Mexico highways. I called the state police to verify the story. They verified it, but still I took off. Outside Vaughan I was picked up by two men who, I was soon to discover, wanted to kill me. When they pulled off the road into a wooded area I managed to escape and from the top of a hill watched their truck traveling slowly along the highway as they looked for me.

Nineteen eighty-two was the last year I went on the road. Since then I have watched America from car and airplane windows, and twice while stranded on the side of highways. I learned much about the state of the American mind while stranded.

Driving out of Omaha one summer evening about nine years ago, I crossed the Missouri River and raced north in western Iowa, searching for an east-west highway that would lead me home. My radiator had a slow leak, and I stopped periodically to fill it with coolant. A hundred miles north of Omaha the needle on the hot/cold indicator went up all the way on hot. Steam flew from under the hood.

I got out, raised the hood, and began waving an arm to flag down a driver. For nearly an hour I stood and waved. Daylight became dusk that grew into night. Car after car rushed past. Finally one man, surely a knight, stopped and drove me to the police station in a nearby, mid-sized city.

Less than a decade later I was driving through Wisconsin in mid-winter when a tire blew out. I pulled over. My trunk was filled with boxes of books that I transferred to the back seat to get to the jack and spare tire. I am asthmatic and the cold air stimulates asthmatic reaction. I did not have my inhaler and moving the boxes was causing me to breathe heavily. I took out the jack and spare tire, but before jacking up the car, I needed to place rocks in front of the tires to keep the car from rolling.

I was parked on the side of a hill. There were no rocks close by, but I saw many at the bottom of the snow-covered slope. I made my way down, across clumps of grass, and found two rocks that weighed about twenty pounds each. I put one under each arm and began trudging back uphill. Halfway up the steep slope I had to drop one of the rocks and pause to get my breath. I was trying to breathe deeply, to suck in enough air to stop the attack. I could not. I was frightened, yet I had to continue to try and put on the spare tire. I brought the rock to the car and, still struggling for breath, dumped it on the ground.

I needed help. I could not stand upright. I began waving at motorists as car after car whizzed by. Why did they not stop? What could they be afraid of? How frightening could an old man with white hair be, especially one who could not stand up straight from trying to suck in air? As in western Iowa ten years earlier, I waited a long time before a man pulled over to help.

Clearly Americans have changed in the last few decades. I could have died of an asthmatic attack, fallen alongside my car, and still I am sure that few would have stopped. Perhaps drivers would think the prostrate man was merely feigning, hoping to trick a passing motorist into stopping and, when he did stop, clobber him with a tire iron.

***

Fear is something Americans today know well. And with fear and distrust so prevalent, far fewer youths now travel on quests for meaning as we in the sixties did. My friends and I believed we could write our futures, whatever futures we wanted, but what future do most youth now see as theirs? How can one seek experience if that experience leads nowhere? How can it, when the faces and voices on radio, television and Internet project only fragments, bits and pieces of people? Lacking also the stimulation of imaginative literature, how does one develop hunger for life?

My hunger to know other peoples and their ways of living was an essential motive powering my journeys across America. But so was my search for a place in this society, if indeed I belonged to it. American society, after all, was in turmoil, its culture confused and violent. America was powered by what many called the System or the Establishment, and many thousands my age shared my anger and contempt for it.

I had no coherent understanding of the world, but neither did the millions of Americans who no longer accepted religious teachings. The intellectual world, like the body politic, was in turmoil. Unlike our ancestors worldwide, who inhabited a cosmos and knew their place within it, most self-styled educated twentieth century Americans saw all life as an alien presence in a hostile world.

Our ancestors, whatever sector of the earth they inhabited, lived with far fewer fractures than we in the sixties. But for most who could not accept the easy pronouncements of fundamentalists and cultists, modernism taught there was no cosmos, no order, no universal frame. Peoples worldwide lost the worlds that gave them presence here and now, and in a hereafter. The moral certainty of each world culture gave way to relativism, and as it did so, the modernist laughed sardonically.

My own quest to find an American soul—an American unity—gave way to an understanding of the fragmentation that is America. The simplicity of a man like Manuel Chavez is no longer possible. News of our wrecked civilization filters down into Duran, into the thousands of dust blown villages across the Great Plains and the Midwest. Today, men like Hal or Gene West—men and women who size up the world for themselves—are looked upon as aberrations, and a man who tried streaking down Washington Avenue today would, very likely, be handcuffed—possibly beaten.

***

Elizabeth and I arrived in Douglas in late June and lived in a cottage overlooking Lake Michigan for a long, golden summer. In early August Elizabeth's brother-in-law came to our cottage to tell us that Nixon was about to make an announcement. We watched him read his resignation speech, walk to the helicopter on the White House grounds, turn and raise both hands above his head in a victory sign. Then he was gone, having put a period to the 1960s.

EPILOGUE

As the sixties wore painfully on, Americans became increasingly divided. The Civil Rights, hippie, and anti-war movements, each pitted one segment of American society against another. In that era of great turbulence we saw the assassinations of John Kennedy, Robert Kennedy, and Martin Luther King. We witnessed white policemen turn water hoses and dogs on blacks. We read about blacks rioting in cities across America and of student takeovers of university campuses. We saw footage of Ohio State Guardsmen murder unarmed student anti-war protestors. The veneer of civilization was thin indeed.

With Richard Nixon's resignation the sixties came to an end. The Vietnam War was over; Civil Rights legislation, including affirmative action, had been enacted. Blacks were now able to compete (in law) on an equal footing with whites. Affirmative action ensured that large numbers of blacks could now enter college. With colleges and universities open to greater numbers of blacks, and with hiring quotas in place, blacks could get jobs with large corporations. The black middle class expanded.

With Nixon gone and Gerald Ford in the White House, the comfort of mediocrity quieted the country. Americans regrouped, worked, felt a more secure future. But we were still shaken by a war we had lost. We had been defeated in Vietnam as we had, in effect, been defeated in Korea. There we had pulled out under truce as Chinese forces massed on the border between the two Koreas. Facing impeachment, Nixon chose to resign. We witnessed the leader of a corrupt administration leaving Washington in disgrace. Just as the last Americans fleeing Vietnam were carried off in helicopters, so was Nixon coptered off White House grounds. The sixties were over but beneath the surface of American life, the violence of the sixties reverberated.

***

The idea of America is a beautiful idea. In concept I believe it to be the most beautiful idea ever conceived by Man. A generation of extraordinary men, deeply learned in philosophy, law, literature and history, managed to create the most remarkable political experiment in human history. But such is the nature of the human species that in little over two centuries following its birth, the idea was corrupted and destroyed by legions of lesser men, until today the United States is controlled politically and financially by some of the lowest elements of humanity.

The energy that propelled the youthful idealism of the early sixties died with the Vietnam War. Much else died too. Gore Vidal likened our Vietnam adventure to the Athenian army's Sicilian Expedition, in which Athens lost two armies and its position as a Mediterranean power. As a result of its defeat in Vietnam, America has tried to control world events with a series of disastrous post-Vietnam adventures: two invasions of Iraq and one in Afghanistan. Our failure in all three attacks have left American prestige in tatters and exposed the futility of armed aggression. As the 76th verse of the *Tao Te Ching* says, When a plant is young it is pliant, when old it is rigid. Rigidity precedes death. The American response to any foreign crisis is force. America is no longer capable of adapting to changing circumstances; it is no longer flexible, no longer inventive.

***

The dream of America is best expressed for me in the writings of Emerson, Whitman, and Lincoln. For me these men proclaim what is deepest in America. The call of Whitman and Lincoln resonates powerfully within me. America, wrote Lincoln, "is the last, great hope of earth. . ." For Whitman, who loved Lincoln, America was the fulfillment of history. Whitman's vision of a land of comrades, men and women, is a call to live life at its fullest. But in his old age, Whitman conceded that his dream was not to be fulfilled. And Emerson approaching old age lost his vision of the transcendent nature of reality and came down to earth to proclaim the glory of American commerce.

Lewis Mumford termed mid-nineteenth century America—the age of Emerson, Whitman, and Melville—America's Golden Age. It was not only the high point of American literature, but a time of philosophical idealism. In our corrupt society I find solace and refuge in the writings of Whitman, Emerson, and Lincoln. In their works the idea of America is revived. Were I to absorb the world's interminable chatter—factoids spit at us endlessly from radios, television, the Internet, newspapers and magazines—I would surely despair. But Emerson and Whitman remind me that the world's chatter is inconsequential, that the universal self is within all, and in that recognition lies Whitman's brotherhood and land of camarados.